SPIRITUAL

GIFTS

SPIRITUAL

GIFTS

Practical teaching and inspirational
accounts of God's supernatural gifts
to His church

David K. Bernard

Spiritual Gifts

by David K. Bernard

©1997 David K. Bernard
Hazelwood, MO 63042-2299

Cover photography and design by Paul Povolni

Unless otherwise indicated, all quotations of Scripture are from the New King James Version (NKJV), copyright 1979, 1980, 1982 by Thomas Nelson Inc., Publishers. Some Scripture quotations are from the King James Version (KJV), and some Scripture quotations are from the New International Version (NIV), copyright 1973, 1978, 1984 by International Bible Society.

Printed in United States of America.

Printed by

Library of Congress Cataloging-in-Publication Data

Bernard, David K., 1956–
    Spiritual gifts / David K. Bernard
       p. cm.
    ISBN 1-56722-204-8
      I. Gifts, Spiritual. 2. Oneness Pentecostal churches—Doctrines.
      3. Pentecostal churches—Doctrines. I. Title.
BT767.3.B39   1997
234'.13—dc21
                                     97-33496
                                        CIP

To
the saints at
New Life
United Pentecostal Church
Austin, Texas

CONTENTS

PREFACE

One of the distinctives of the Pentecostal movement is its emphasis on the supernatural gifts of the Spirit at work in the church today. In the latter half of the twentieth century, many people from every denomination embraced these gifts, giving rise to the charismatic movement and then to the "third wave" (evangelicals who do not identify themselves as Pentecostals or charismatics but who advocate signs and wonders). Diverse theories and practices, including some misuse and abuse, have accompanied this renewal of spiritual gifts.

The purpose of this book is to articulate a biblical theology of the supernatural gifts of I Corinthians 12 for all who embrace the miraculous work of the Holy Spirit. Using Scripture as our authority, we will attempt to define the spiritual gifts, investigate their nature, and discuss their proper function and use.

While experience must not be our authority, it serves a vital role in developing a practical understanding of this subject. At the beginning of the twentieth century, the early Pentecostals discovered the biblical teaching about the baptism of the Holy Spirit, speaking in tongues, and the gifts of the Spirit, and they sought to receive and implement these truths. As God poured out His Spirit with signs following, what they once found obscure, mysterious, or merely theoretical suddenly became a clear and living reality. As they followed the leading of the Spirit, they corrected misconceptions and abuses by referring back to the Bible and its explanation of the purpose and operation of spiritual gifts.

We must do the same today. We must interpret all experiences by the Bible and base all practices upon the Bible. At the same time, we analyze our theories about the meaning of God's Word by examining the ongoing work of the Holy Spirit in the world, the church, and our daily lives. The interaction between our theories and our experiences will help us understand and recapture the full, true meaning of the biblical text. Thus equipped, we will be able to conform our beliefs and practices to God's will as revealed in Scripture.

In this connection, I have been extremely blessed to have a rich Apostolic Pentecostal heritage and an unusual diversity of experiences that have helped give perspective to this subject. Beginning in 1965, my parents served as missionaries to Korea for over twenty years, and they established churches in Louisiana before and after their foreign service. I grew up in home and foreign missions amid revival, miracles, signs, wonders, and church growth.

Upon my return to the United States at age seventeen to attend college, I became part of a large, multicultural church in the heart of Houston and later a small church in Austin, Texas. I began full-time Christian ministry in 1981, first being associated with a Bible college and a large church in Jackson, Mississippi, and next with the world headquarters of the United Pentecostal Church

International and a medium-sized church in suburban St. Louis. In 1992 my wife and I founded a church in Austin, where as pastor I have watched it grow from our home to a rented building shared with another group to its own facilities of thirteen thousand square feet on four acres of land.

As of 1997, I have had the opportunity of visiting fifty-eight countries, taking twenty-seven short-term missions trips, and ministering in twenty-eight countries on five continents. I have visited all fifty states of the Union, preaching and teaching in forty-two. In total, I have ministered in approximately 245 churches or cities in the United States and 75 in other countries, including various conferences, retreats, seminars, youth camps, and camp meetings.

My purpose in mentioning these facts is not to bring credit to myself or to make great claims but to disclose my background and variety of experience so that I can be a credible and effective witness of what I proclaim. I have been privileged to see all the supernatural spiritual gifts in operation repeatedly in numerous cultures and settings, both home and foreign, from small house groups to crowds in domed stadiums. Throughout the book, I cite examples from my own observation and experience, not to imply that I am somehow special but just the opposite: to testify first-hand that all believers and ministers today can experience the supernatural gifts of the Spirit.

The initial outline for this book arose from teaching systematic theology for five years at Jackson College of Ministries in Jackson, Mississippi. The rough draft was transcribed from an extension class of Texas Bible College taught on the premises of Concordia University in Austin. Unless otherwise indicated, Scripture quotations are from the New King James Version (NKJV) and definitions of English words are from *The American Heritage Dictionary*.

I wish to thank Claire Borne for the initial typing and my mother, Loretta Bernard, for contributing experiences and suggestions. As always, I thank my wife, Connie Bernard, for her patience, support, and invaluable contributions in numerous ways to my life, family, and ministry.

I do not write as an expert in spiritual gifts but as one who believes that every Christian can obtain a working knowledge of these gifts from the Bible itself, that every Spirit-filled person can potentially exercise any of them as God wills and enables, and that God intends for them to operate within every local body of believers.

CHAPTER ONE

SPIRITUAL GIFTS IN THE BIBLE

The Bible teaches that every believer is, and should function as, a vital part of the body of Christ. God has bestowed many gifts upon His church. He has endowed the members with special abilities and ministries for the benefit of the body as a whole, both locally and worldwide.

Three passages in the New Testament—Romans 12, Ephesians 4, and I Corinthians 12—list some gifts that God has granted the church. Romans 12 discusses abilities, talents, or functions that God gives to all believers. Ephesians 4 identifies special offices of leadership and ministry that God has given to the church. In I Corinthians 12 we find supernatural signs, wonders, and miracles that occur by the direct operation and power of the Holy Spirit. For the sake of clarity, we will label these three lists respectively as the service gifts, the ministerial office gifts, and the supernatural gifts. In this chapter we will discuss the service gifts and ministerial office gifts; the remainder of the book will be devoted to the supernatural spiritual gifts of I Corinthians 12-14.

The three lists of gifts are as follows:

The Service Gifts *(Romans 12:6-8)*
1. Prophecy
2. Ministry
3. Teaching
4. Exhortation
5. Giving
6. Leading (ruling in KJV)
7. Showing mercy

The Ministerial Office Gifts *(Ephesians 4:11)*
1. Apostles
2. Prophets
3. Evangelists
4. Pastors
5. Teachers

The Supernatural Spiritual Gifts *(I Corinthians 12:8-10)*
1. Word of wisdom
2. Word of knowledge
3. Faith
4. Gifts of healings
5. Working of miracles
6. Prophecy
7. Discerning of spirits
8. Different kinds of tongues
9. Interpretation of tongues

We also find in I Corinthians 12:28-30 a list that combines elements from each of the preceding categories:

1. Apostles
2. Prophets
3. Teachers
4. Miracles (also "workers of miracles," verse 29)
5. Gifts of healings
6. Helps (similar to "ministry")
7. Administrations ("governments" in KJV, similar to leading or ruling)
8. Varieties of tongues
9. Interpretation of tongues (verse 30).

THE SERVICE GIFTS

"For I say, through the grace given to me, to everyone who is among you, not to think of himself more highly than he ought to think, but to think soberly, as God has dealt to each one a measure of faith. For as we have many members in one body, but all the members do not have the same function, so we, being many, are one body in Christ, and individually members of one another. Having then gifts differing according to the grace that is given to us, let us use them: if prophecy, let us prophesy in proportion to our faith; or ministry, let us use it in our ministering; he who teaches, in teaching; he who exhorts, in exhortation; he who gives, with liberality; he who leads, with diligence; he who shows mercy, with cheerfulness" (Romans 12:3-8).

In this passage, Paul spoke by the grace given to him, namely, in virtue of his divine calling as an apostle. In doing so he himself became an example of his message. His inspired message to each individual believer is: we must be humble, recognizing that God is the author of everything we achieve spiritually. We must not value ourselves too highly, but we must think with sober judgment.

We are to make this serious estimation in accordance with the faith God has given us. We have no cause for esteeming ourselves higher than others when we realize that God is the source of our faith and that God has given faith to everyone in the church.

We must seek to identify our particular gifts.

As an analogy, the human body has many parts, but not all these members have the same function. There is one body but many members—one body but different functions. Similarly, the church is the body of Christ, and Christians are all members of that one body. (See also I Corinthians 12:12-27.) Thus each one is part of the others; each is mutually dependent on one another.

The different members of the church have different offices and gifts, just as body parts have different functions. For this reason we dare not compare ourselves among ourselves (II Corinthians 10:12), but we should recognize a diversity of functions and acknowledge the value of the various members of the body. We must seek to identify our particular gifts and exercise them to the best of our ability for the benefit of the body as a whole. Instead of seeking to do every possible task in the body, we should concentrate on the particular functions God has given us and perform them well.

> *We should concentrate on the particular functions God has given us and perform them well.*

The Greek word for "gifts" here is *charismata*, the plural of *charisma*. It is also used of the nine spiritual gifts of I Corinthians 12. This word is related to *charis*, or "grace," which refers to the free, undeserved blessing and work of God. The connotation is that these gifts are free, unmerited, miraculous endowments from God.

In the context, Paul cited seven examples of his thesis. His manner of presentation reveals that the list of gifts here is not exhaustive but representative or illustrative of the ways God uses individuals in His church. There are many other aspects of Christian service that this passage does not specifically identify.

We may also describe these service gifts as spiritual functions or ministries (avenues of service) in the church. One person can exercise several of them, and there can be some overlap.

These are truly gifts from God and not merely human

attainments. While there are some natural human abilities that correspond to this list, at least in part, even the talents we receive from nature and nurture have their ultimate source in the design, purpose, and grace of God. Moreover, God's work of grace in the Christian enables him to exercise his abilities in the spiritual realm and for the benefit of the church, transcending his carnal human capacity. God may sanctify, build upon, and add to talents he already had before he came to God, or God may give him completely new talents. Either way, these gifts come by the grace of God.

The first in the list, *prophecy*, means a divinely inspired utterance, or speaking under divine unction to edify others. It does not necessarily involve a prediction of the future. It can refer specifically to a supernatural public message in the language of the audience (I Corinthians 14:29-31), but here it seems to have the more general meaning of anointed testimony, proclamation, or preaching. (See Acts 2:17; I Corinthians 14:3; Revelation 19:10.) Lay preachers, including those who speak at services in various institutions such as jails and nursing homes, are a good example of this gift in operation.

If someone has this gift, he should exercise it in proportion to his faith—as much as his measure of faith will enable him. Perhaps this statement means he should testify or preach in agreement with the faith (the doctrine or body of belief).

Ministry means service to others, particularly service in the church. Some people are especially gifted with an attitude and ability of service in certain capacities. The

Greek word is *diakonia*, which is a broad word that covers a variety of service, work, or assistance. It can also refer specifically to the work of a deacon, who helps with the business and organizational matters in a local church. (See Acts 6:1-6; I Timothy 3:8-13.)

Then there is the gift of *teaching*, or instruction. Home Bible study teachers and Sunday school teachers are modern examples of people who operate this gift.

Exhortation means giving encouragement or comfort. Some people exercise this gift by public testimony, while others do so primarily by personal contact of various forms including friendship, telephone calls, letters, and cards. Joses was so well-known for this gift that the apostles gave him the surname Barnabas, meaning "Son of Encouragement." (See Acts 4:36; 9:26-27.)

The gift of *giving* is sharing material blessings with others and with the church. The KJV says to give with "simplicity," but most commentators understand the underlying Greek word to mean "liberality, generosity." It can also mean "singleness of heart, sincere concern." Some people are blessed significantly more than others with the means and opportunity to give to God's cause. They should not consider their material blessings to be a sign of superiority but a gift of God for the purpose of assisting His kingdom in a special way. They should not be selfish but generous, recognizing that in God's plan they have greater ability and responsibility to give than most others.

Leading, or ruling in the KJV, speaks of direction, guidance, and influence within the church. Leaders are to exercise their role with diligence, carefulness, and earnestness. God has ordained rulers or leaders in His church. It is important to submit to human authority in the church (Hebrews 13:17), as long as human leaders exercise their authority under God according to the guidelines of His Word. The church needs various people with leadership and administrative ability. In addition to the pastor and pastoral staff, the successful congregation will have capable leaders over various departments and activities as well as influential opinion makers and role models who may or may not have an official position.

Showing mercy means being merciful and kind to others. It can include visiting the sick, helping the poor, and assisting widows and orphans. (See Matthew 25:31-46; Galatians 2:10; James 1:27; 2:15-17.) A person who fills this role should do it cheerfully, not in a begrudging, mournful, or patronizing way.

To some extent, every mature Christian should be able to function in the seven areas just listed.

To some extent, every mature Christian should be able to function in the seven areas just listed. All Christians are to be an effective witness, to serve, to encourage, to give, and to show mercy. All should have some basic ability to instruct unbelievers in the plan of salvation and to lead new converts in the ways of the Lord. This passage tells us, however, that each Christian has some area of special strength, given by God. While we should always "be ready for every good work" (Titus 3:1), we need to discern what our strong points are and use them effectively.

To summarize, each Christian has a particular gift, role, or function in the church, or possibly several of them. Whatever God has given him to do, he should exercise it to his full capacity but always with humility.

THE MINISTERIAL OFFICE GIFTS

"Therefore He says: 'When He ascended on high, He led captivity captive, and gave gifts to men.' . . . And He Himself gave some to be apostles, some prophets, some evangelists, and some pastors and teachers, for the equipping of the saints for the work of ministry, for the edifying of the body of Christ, till we all come to the unity of the faith and the knowledge of the Son of God, to a perfect man, to the measure of the stature of the fullness of Christ; that we should no longer be children, tossed to and fro and carried about with every wind of doctrine, by the trickery of men, in the cunning craftiness by which they lie in wait to deceive, but, speaking the truth in love, may grow up in all things into Him who is the head— Christ—from whom the whole body, joined and knit together by what every joint supplies, according to the effective working by which every part does its share, causes growth of the body for the edifying of itself in love" (Ephesians 4:8, 11-16).

This passage introduces what is often called the five-fold ministry. The five ministries listed are not simply God's gifts to individuals within the church, but they are God's gifts (Greek, *domata*) to the church as a whole. While Romans 12 speaks of abilities or functions, using both nouns and verbs to describe the operation of the service gifts, Ephesians 4 speaks of offices, using nouns to designate them. The indication is that the gifts of Ephesians 4 are more formal or defined ministries in and for the whole church. When Jesus ascended to heaven He gave gifts to the church—the ministers of the gospel.

The people who hold these offices are recognized leaders in the church, responsible for equipping others.

As the passage reveals, the people who hold these offices are recognized leaders in the church, responsible for equipping others and thereby helping the church to function effectively, grow into maturity, and become established in doctrinal truth. The nature of their work requires that they be preachers of the gospel. In modern terminology, we typically call them ministers, using this designation in a special sense, even though in the KJV and NKJV the term *minister* is a general one signifying a servant or worker.

The word "some" appears four times in verse 11, separately modifying "apostles," "prophets," and "evangelists" but modifying "pastors and teachers" as a unit. The implication is that the same person fills both the role of pastor and the role of teacher. Indeed, while the pastor must "do the work of an evangelist" (II Timothy 4:5), his primary ministry of the Word is teaching. He must be "able to teach" (I Timothy 3:2; II Timothy 2:24). Some ministers have a more specialized calling and ability to teach, but all pastors must also be teachers.

An *apostle* (Greek, *apostolos*) is literally someone sent with a commission, messenger, ambassador, commissioner. Although no one can take the place of the twelve apostles of the Lamb (Revelation 21:14), who were eyewitnesses of Christ, others fulfill an apostolic office by serving as pioneer missionaries and leaders of other ministers.

For instance, the church at Antioch sent Paul and Barnabas as pioneer missionaries, and they became known as apostles even though neither were part of the Twelve. (See Acts 13:2-4; 14:14; I Corinthians 9:2.) Likewise, James the Lord's brother was an apostle (Galatians 1:19). Although he was not one of the Twelve, he was the leader of the church in Jerusalem. (See Acts 15:13; 21:18.) Andronicus and Junia apparently were apostles also (Romans 16:7).

A *prophet* is one who imparts special messages or direction from God. (See Acts 11:27; 15:32; 21:10.) While many people in the church may prophesy from time to time, the office of a prophet is filled by someone whom God consistently uses in this manner in his public ministry. All preachers should preach the Word of God

23

and preach under the anointing of the Holy Spirit, but the prophet is specially called and enabled to proclaim the specific will, purpose, and counsel of God to His people. He will frequently communicate messages concerning God's plan for the future or the church's need to take action in God's plan.

We should recognize, encourage, and heed apostolic and prophetic ministries in our midst.

From the examples in the Book of Acts, it is evident that the offices of apostle and prophet are for the church at all times. Over the centuries, many false apostles and prophets have arisen, claiming these titles in an attempt to assert supreme authority in the church (I John 4:1; Revelation 2:2). The Bible is our sole authority for salvation and Christian living, however, and those who proclaim any other gospel are accursed (Galatians 1:8-9; II Timothy 3:15-17). Therefore, it may not be wise for someone to claim to be an apostle or prophet, or for others to promote him as such. Even so, we should recognize, encourage, and heed apostolic and prophetic ministries in our midst.

An *evangelist* is literally a preacher of the gospel. He proclaims the good news for the benefit of the unsaved. (See Acts 21:8; II Timothy 4:5.) This biblical term is not limited to the modern usage of an itinerant preacher who holds special services. Rather, it connotes a minister who is particularly effective in winning souls, whether individually or in public preaching.

A *pastor* (literally, "shepherd") is one who leads and takes care of God's people. The Bible also speaks of him as a bishop (literally, "overseer") and an elder. (See Acts 14:23; 20:17, 28; I Timothy 3:1-7; Titus 1:5-9.)

I Peter 5:1-4 describes the pastor's role of leading, overseeing, and instructing the believers under his care: "The elders who are among you I exhort, I who am a fellow elder and a witness of the sufferings of Christ, and also a partaker of the glory that will be revealed: Shepherd the flock of God which is among you, serving as overseers, not by constraint, but willingly, not for dishonest gain but eagerly; nor as being lords over those entrusted to you, but being examples to the flock; and when the Chief Shepherd appears, you will receive the crown of glory that does not fade away."

The New Testament always speaks of elders in the plural, indicating that in each city the church was led by a pastoral team. Scripture, history, and common sense all indicate that there was a senior pastor or presiding elder. (See Revelation 2-3, in which Jesus addressed a letter to the "angel," literally "messenger," of each of seven churches in Asia Minor.) Today we may think of the elders of the church in a city as the senior pastor and pastoral staff of a local church, or as the pastors of various congregations in one city who cooperate as part of the same organization.

A *teacher* is one who instructs in God's Word. (See Acts 13:1.) As we have seen, in this context it specifically describes the preaching and teaching role of an overseer in a local church. While many people in the church may have the gift of teaching and can teach effectively in various settings, such as Sunday school classes and home Bible studies, the office of pastor-teacher stands above them. The pastor-teacher is the leading preacher and teacher of the Word. God has not only given him the gift of teaching, but God has given him to the church as its teacher and overseer.

Verse 12 explains the purpose for which God gave apostles, prophets, evangelists, pastors and teachers to the church. The commas in this verse in the KJV could lead someone to interpret it as describing three separate tasks of these ministers, but punctuation was not part of the original text of Scripture. Translators added punctuation to aid in reading and comprehension. In this case, a study of the Greek text and various translations makes it clear that there is one purpose with a threefold progression, as follows:

1. God gives the ministerial offices to the church for the "perfecting" (KJV) or "equipping" (NKJV) of the believers.

2. The saints are equipped so they can do "the work of ministry." Here "ministry" means "service," or all the functions of the church. Every believer should have a ministry—not necessarily a public preaching ministry but a specific place of service in the body of Christ. It is the task of the apostles, prophets, evangelists, pastors and teachers to help each saint find his work of ministry and train him to perform that task properly within the body.

Those who hold the five ministerial offices are to inspire, motivate, disciple, instruct, and prepare the saints so that everyone is an active, productive member of the body.

3. When each member of the body performs his proper function, the whole body will be edified, or built up. The goal is to attain maturity in Christ. Beginning with "the unity of the Spirit in the bond of peace" (Ephesians 4:3), we are to pursue "the unity of the faith and the knowledge of the Son of God, to a perfect man, to the measure of the stature of the fullness of Christ" (Ephesians 4:13).

According to Ephesians 4:14-16, each local body of believers should seek several specific characteristics in their growth toward maturity:

1. Becoming established in the faith so that they are not swayed by false doctrine and false leaders.

2. Speaking the truth in love. They learn to minister to one another and to unbelievers with a balance of honesty and compassion, equally valuing and manifesting truth and love.

3. Submitting to the lordship of Jesus Christ in all things and depending upon His divine supply for all things.

4. Everyone learning to contribute his or her share to the work of the church, so that the body can grow and be built up in love.

Summary

The service gifts of Romans 12 exemplify how God gives each member of the church one or more special abilities to function productively in the body. The ministerial office gifts of Ephesians 4 are God's endowment to the local and worldwide church for the purpose of equipping the members for their assigned tasks.

In addition, God has given the church the supernatural spiritual gifts of I Corinthians 12 as miraculous signs to attest to the work of the church and as miraculous empowerings to further the work of the church. We now turn our attention to these gifts of revelation, power, and utterance.

CHAPTER TWO

THE SUPERNATURAL SPIRITUAL GIFTS

"Now concerning spiritual gifts, brethren, I do not want you to be ignorant. . . . There are diversities of gifts, but the same Spirit. There are differences of ministries, but the same Lord. And there are diversities of activities, but it is the same God who works all in all. But the manifestation of the Spirit is given to each one for the profit of all: for to one is given the word of wisdom through the Spirit, to another the word of knowledge through the same Spirit, to another faith by the same Spirit, to another gifts of healings by the same Spirit, to another the working of miracles, to another prophecy, to another discerning of spirits, to another different kinds of tongues, to another the interpretation of tongues. But one and the same Spirit works all these things, distributing to each one individually as He wills" (I Corinthians 12:1, 4-11).

I Corinthians 12 speaks of "gifts" as miraculous endowments that operate by the power of the Holy Spirit. Let us look at the character of these supernatural spiritual gifts.

THE ORIGIN OF THE GIFTS

We must first understand that the originator of these gifts is the Holy Spirit. The Spirit is God Himself with particular reference to His spiritual essence and spiritual action. (See Genesis 1:1-2; John 4:24.) In this context, the Spirit is God at work in human lives.

I Corinthians 12:4-7 makes clear that God is the source of these gifts. While the gifts differ and their manner of administration varies, the one true God is the author of them all. God is the one who gives them, and God is the one who performs the work.

THE SUPERNATURAL CHARACTER OF THE GIFTS

Specifically, these gifts are supernatural. This passage describes them as "works" of God and as the "manifestation of the Spirit." A manifestation is a demonstration or display; the verb "manifest" means to reveal or show plainly.

Thus it is a mistake to define these gifts in terms of natural human abilities as some commentators, who do not believe in miracles today, attempt to do. For instance, they define the word of wisdom as having good judgment and counseling ability, the gifts of healing as the ability to be a good doctor or nurse, and the gift of tongues as the ability to learn foreign languages well. But according to such definitions, someone who has never felt God's presence, much less received God's Spirit, could exercise these gifts as effectively as believers.

Of course, in a general sense, all abilities and talents come from God. He created humans in His image as spiritual, moral, intellectual beings with all the qualities that this description entails. But this passage does not merely speak generally of gifts that flow from the grace of God (as we might maintain regarding the service gifts in Romans 12). Rather, I Corinthians 12 focuses on the supernatural by describing these gifts as "spiritual."

Hebrews 2:3-4 underscores the supernatural character of the "gifts of the Holy Spirit": "How shall we escape if we neglect so great a salvation, which at the first began to be spoken by the Lord, and was confirmed to us by those who heard Him, God also bearing witness both with signs and wonders, with various miracles, and gifts of the Holy Spirit, according to His own will?"

The gift of tongues is a good example. The discussion in I Corinthians 14 clearly reveals that it is not a gift of learning languages but a gift of speaking miraculously in languages that neither the speaker nor the audience understands.

GIVEN ACCORDING TO THE WILL OF GOD

Understanding the supernatural origin and character of these gifts is vital to identify them accurately and exercise them properly. For instance, a charismatic group advertised that it was conducting a school on prophecy. It promised to teach every student how to prophesy and further promised that every student would receive a personal prophecy before the end of the seminar.

If the gifts operate according to God's administration, however, how can humans guarantee who will exercise specific gifts and when they will do so? There is great value in learning about the spiritual gifts and learning to yield to God's Spirit so that we are prepared for God to use us. It is presumptuous to suggest, however, that any human can grant such a gift to someone or exercise such a gift at will. We cannot teach anyone to prophesy or work miracles. We can teach people how to be available for God's Spirit to work through them, but we must always recognize that God is the one who bestows and enables the gifts according to His sovereign purpose. (See I Corinthians 12:11; Hebrews 2:4.)

The spiritual gifts originate
in the mind and power of God.

We can pray with people and assure them that God will hear and respond. We can pray for God's direction and then share with an individual whatever God discloses to us. In doing so, however, we must be careful to keep the focus on God and His will.

As chapter 4 discusses, we are channels of God's

Spirit, and He expects us to exercise the gifts according to His Word. We must regulate ourselves lest we misuse the gifts. (See I Corinthians 14:32.) Our will plays an important part in the exercise of spiritual gifts, but we must always remember that they originate in the mind and power of God.

The most important consideration is not our will, but God's.

The most important consideration is not our will, but God's. When we pray for someone, we must pray according to God's will. If someone is sick, for example, it is God's will for us to pray for him, for the Bible instructs us to do so. (See James 5:14.) We cannot guarantee healing in the manner and time that the person may desire, however, unless we hear specifically from God. What we can promise, based on God's Word, is that God will hear our prayer, and God will help us. We are to pray and believe God for healing, but we cannot dictate the precise way in which God chooses to work.

Many times God answers with an instantaneous miracle, but in other cases He does not. Either way, God is at work. If He does not deliver a person immediately from his or her trial, He will give grace sufficient to endure. (See I Corinthians 10:13; II Corinthians 12:8-10.) In both instances, God responds positively to prayer. Even if He says no to a specific request, He will give the grace and strength to accomplish His will in the circumstances.

In sum, we should not focus on our performance of a notable deed but rather on our being a vessel and a channel for God to do whatever He wants to do in a given situation. It is not necessarily our responsibility to understand the reasons for God's answer, but it is our responsibility to keep praying, believing, and pressing on until victory comes.

Since the spiritual gifts are from God, we should draw attention to what God is doing, not what humans are doing. It is troubling when the primary emphasis is on "John Doe Ministries" or the exercise of particular gifts. It is likewise troubling when people promote a gift such as healing, prophecy, or word of knowledge as an end in itself or as a means of exalting a preacher's reputation instead of promoting the divine purpose behind the gifts. For instance, the gifts of healing are often quite effective in building faith and sparking a revival that leads many people to salvation. (See, for example, Acts 3:1-11; 4:4.) But if a meeting or a ministry focuses on healing while neglecting the message of salvation, then God's purpose in granting healing is not fully accomplished.

GIVEN FOR TIMES OF SPECIAL NEED

God grants the spiritual gifts of I Corinthians 12 for times of special need or crisis. In the church, the supernatural gifts should be normal, not abnormal; expected, not unexpected. They do not operate continually, however. If they did, we would not think of them as supernatural.

To illustrate, in the Gospels and Acts multitudes were healed and a number of people were raised from the dead. Nevertheless, all the members of the early church eventually died without being raised again, and presumably most died of some illness or disease that was not healed. The gifts of healing and working of miracles were common, but they did not occur in every situation.

The supernatural gifts should be normal, not abnormal; expected, not unexpected. They do not operate continually, however.

Jesus undoubtedly passed the lame man at the Temple gate many times but did not heal him on those occasions; instead he was healed when he encountered Peter and John in Acts 3. While God raised Dorcas from the dead in Acts 9, He did not raise up the apostle James, who was executed in Acts 12.

As another example, the "word of wisdom" is a "word," or a portion, of divine wisdom. It does not operate in a person's life for twenty-four hours a day, but it is a special revelation for a specific time. No one can know all the mind of God all the time, but at a special time of need He sometimes imparts a portion of His supernatural wisdom to an individual.

I Corinthians 14 provides guidelines for speaking in

tongues, teaching that in public gatherings only two or three people should address the congregation in tongues. Likewise, only two or three people should speak prophetically in one meeting. We should expect these supernatural utterances in our worship services; they should not surprise us. Nevertheless, God does not intend for them to operate continually in a given meeting or to dominate a meeting. They are special gifts at a particular moment for a specific purpose.

NATURAL LIFE, SPIRITUAL LIFE, AND SPIRITUAL GIFTS

As we examine the supernatural character of these gifts, we must distinguish them from natural human qualities that may correspond to them in some measure as well as from spiritual principles that operate in the everyday life of all Christians. For instance, we can distinguish three levels of wisdom. First, humans can have wisdom in the natural realm even without a relationship with God. (See Luke 16:8; I Corinthians 2:4-6.) An atheist can be wise in planning his career, and a criminal can make wise preparations in conducting his sinful deeds. Of course, in a spiritual sense such a person is not wise but foolish.

Second, there is wisdom in the spiritual realm, which all believers possess to some extent and which should guide all their conduct. God imparts wisdom to all the righteous, to everyone who seeks it. (See Proverbs 2:6-7; James 1:5.) While spiritual wisdom as a daily guide for

Christian living is thus a gift from God, it is not the supernatural spiritual gift mentioned in I Corinthians 12, which speaks of special manifestations or empowerings that God grants certain individuals at certain times, not to everyone all the time.

Third, as we have seen, there is "the word of wisdom." In contrast to the natural wisdom of everyday human life or the spiritual wisdom of everyday Christian life, it is a supernatural gift of a portion of God's wisdom in a particular situation.

Likewise, we can observe three levels of knowledge: worldly or human knowledge, spiritual knowledge, and "the word of knowledge."

As a further example, there is the faith of everyday life, which sinners place in themselves, others, material possessions, traditions, or false gods, but which they need to place in the true God for salvation. (See I Corinthians 2:5; Hebrews 11:6.) The Bible also speaks of faith (Greek, *pistis*) as part of "the fruit of the Spirit" (Galatians 5:22). In this sense, faith is the daily trust, reliance, fidelity, and "faithfulness" (NKJV) that God's Spirit develops in believers and that is characteristic of every mature Christian. Yet I Corinthians 12 speaks of a special "gift of faith" that not all Christians receive. While the Spirit is the source of both the "fruit" and the "gift," the former term describes a quality that develops in the normal process of growing as a Christian, just as an apple tree naturally bears apples, while the latter term describes a direct intervention from outside a Christian's own resources, just as a person receives a gift from a friend.

We may not be able to identify three analogous levels for every spiritual gift, but these examples show that we must understand the gifts of I Corinthians 12 in the most supernatural, specific sense. While these gifts may have counterparts or parallels in everyday natural life, spiritual life, or both, this passage clearly describes specific manifestations of divine power that God does not give to unbelievers and that He does not give to all believers—at least not the same gifts in the same way to everyone.

This distinction will also become evident as we discuss the gifts of tongues and prophecy. While it is desirable for all Christians to prophesy in the general sense of anointed testimony or exhortation, and while it is desirable for all Christians to speak in tongues as part of their private devotion, not everyone will publicly speak a prophecy, tongue, or interpretation directly inspired by God to a congregation for a certain occasion. Paul wrote, "I wish you all spoke with tongues, but even more that you prophesied. . . . Therefore, brethren, desire earnestly to prophesy, and do not forbid to speak with tongues" (I Corinthians 14:5, 39). He also pointed out, however, "There are diversities of gifts. . . . For to one is given the word of wisdom through the Spirit, . . . to another prophecy . . . to another different kinds of tongues, to another the interpretation of tongues" (I Corinthians 12:4, 8, 10). Thus he asked rhetorically, expecting a negative reply, "Are all prophets? . . . Do all speak with tongues? Do all interpret?" (I Corinthians 12:29-30).

DIVERSITY OF GIFTS

As with Romans 12, it does not appear that the list of gifts in I Corinthians 12 is meant to be exhaustive. Scripture does not assert that all God's miraculous workings in our lives must fall under exactly one of the nine categories of I Corinthians 12:8-10. The chapter presents this list to illustrate how God works supernaturally in different ways using different members of the body.

It also seems that there can be some overlap in the exercise of the gifts. For instance, if God grants someone a word of knowledge and the person then discloses it to someone else, we could describe his utterance as a prophecy. If God gives someone faith in a time of crisis, we may also see the working of miracles as the person exercises his faith.

The main point is to become sensitive, available, and yielded to the move of God's Spirit.

These observations indicate that we do not need to be overly technical in our attempt to define the nine spiritual gifts, nor do we need to be overly concerned about slight variations that teachers may propose in their definitions of them. The main point is not to label what God is doing but to become sensitive, available, and yielded to the move of God's Spirit. Whether we identify a specific instance as "the word of wisdom" or "the word of knowledge" is not of primary importance, as long as we allow God to work through us supernaturally to meet the need in a given situation.

While it is not necessary to pigeonhole every miraculous work of God, we do need a clear understanding of the principles by which God works. Our authority in such matters, as in all aspects of Christian living, is the Bible. (See II Timothy 3:15-17.) We should beware when someone places heavy emphasis on a supernatural manifestation for which there is no biblical precedent or when someone promotes certain techniques that the Bible does not explicitly teach. We certainly cannot treat such cases as normative or urge everyone to follow them. Although not every specific situation will have a biblical parallel, the principles by which God operates will always remain the same. A study of Scripture reveals the characteristics of His work as well as the types of manifestations His church is to expect and seek.

In sum, while we cannot reduce the supernatural manifestations of the Spirit to rigid academic categories, it is important to study the gifts and develop a clear understanding of them from Scripture. As we become more knowledgeable of this subject, we can more easily recognize and respond to God's leading in this area and open ourselves to all the manifestations of the Spirit.

CHAPTER THREE

THE PURPOSE OF SPIRITUAL GIFTS

"But the Helper, the Holy Spirit, whom the Father will send in My name, He will teach you all things, and bring to your remembrance all things that I said to you. . . . But when the Helper comes, whom I shall send to you from the Father, the Spirit of truth who proceeds from the Father, He will testify of Me. . . . And when He has come, He will convict the world of sin, and of righteousness, and of judgment. . . . When He, the Spirit of truth, has come, He will guide you into all truth; for He will not speak on His own authority, but whatever He hears He will speak; and He will tell you things to come. He will glorify Me, for He will take of what is Mine and declare it to you" (John 14:26; 15:26; 16:8, 13-14).

"But the manifestation of the Spirit is given to each one for the profit of all" (I Corinthians 12:7).

"But he who prophesies speaks edification and exhortation and comfort to men" (I Corinthians 14:3).

ULTIMATE PURPOSE

Jesus taught that after His ascension the Holy Spirit would come to dwell within the hearts of believers. (See Luke 24:49; John 7:37-39; 14:16-18; 16:7; Acts 1:4-5.) The Holy Spirit is the "Helper" or "Comforter" (KJV). In the original Greek this title is *parakletos*, which literally means "one called alongside to help," that is, a helper, consoler, or advocate.

According to John 14-16, the Holy Spirit would teach the disciples and guide them into all truth, by causing them to remember and comprehend the teachings of Jesus. The Spirit in them would not become a new source of authority but would impart understanding from the mind of God.

> *The ultimate purpose of the spiritual gifts is to exalt the Lord Jesus Christ.*

Above all, the Spirit testifies of Jesus and glorifies Jesus. He confirms the identity and work of Jesus Christ; proclaims the reality of the Incarnation and the Atonement; demonstrates the saving, delivering, transforming power of the gospel of Jesus Christ; promotes worship of Jesus Christ as Lord and God; and guides believers into the future, preparing them for the return of Jesus for His church.

John 14-16 describes the work of the Holy Spirit in the church today, which, while far broader than the nine gifts of I Corinthians 12, certainly encompasses these gifts. Therefore, we can conclude that *the ultimate purpose of the spiritual gifts is to exalt the Lord Jesus Christ.*

This purpose provides the basis for an important test of spiritual manifestations: "No one speaking by the Spirit of God calls Jesus accursed, and no one can say that Jesus is Lord except by the Holy Spirit" (I Corinthians 12:3).

IMMEDIATE PURPOSE

Immediately before listing the nine spiritual gifts, I Corinthians 12 says they are manifested to individuals for the benefit of the entire church: "But the manifestation of the Spirit is given to each one for the profit of all" (verse 7).

Immediately after listing the nine spiritual gifts, I Corinthians 12 proceeds to describe the church as the body of Christ. The body has many members, and each of them has a different function, but they are all designed to work together for the benefit of the entire body. "For as the body is one and has many members, but all the members of that one body, being many, are one body, so also is Christ. . . . And the eye cannot say to the hand, 'I have no need of you'; nor again the head to the feet, 'I have no need of you.' No, much rather, those members of the body which seem to be weaker are necessary. . . . But God composed

43

the body, having given greater honor to that part which lacks it, that there should be no schism in the body, but that the members should have the same care for one another" (I Corinthians 12:12, 21-22, 24-25).

From this explanation, it is clear that God does not bestow the spiritual gifts primarily to benefit individuals but to benefit the body as a whole. While the gifts do bless individuals, the focus is on what these individuals can then contribute to the church. Moreover, God does not intend for the gifts to work in isolation but to operate together in order to achieve the desired objective.

> *God does not bestow the spiritual gifts primarily to benefit individuals but to benefit the body as a whole.*

In discussing the proper use of the vocal gifts, Paul explained, "But he who prophesies speaks edification and exhortation and comfort to men" (I Corinthians 14:3). While this verse refers specifically to the gift of prophecy, there is a broader principle: The exercise of spiritual gifts should be governed by a consideration of how they benefit others.

This principle extends to a consideration of unbelievers as well as believers. The church is in the process of reaching out to sinners and transforming them into saints. Therefore, in exercising spiritual gifts, we must also take into account the impact upon potential believers. For instance, tongues serves as a valuable sign for the unbeliever, while prophecy helps to convince and convict someone who comes as an unbeliever but then begins to believe because of the miraculous demonstration he observes. (See I Corinthians 14:22-25.) We must recall that part of the work of the Holy Spirit is to "convict the world of sin, and of righteousness, and of judgment" (John 16:8).

> ## The immediate purpose of the supernatural gifts is to edify, or build up, the church.

Spiritual gifts bear witness to and confirm the preaching of the gospel: "And they went out and preached everywhere, the Lord working with them and confirming the word through the accompanying signs" (Mark 16:20). "How shall we escape if we neglect so great a salvation, which at the first began to be spoken by the Lord, and was confirmed to us by those who heard Him, God also bearing witness both with signs and wonders, with various miracles, and gifts of the Holy Spirit, according to His own will?" (Hebrews 2:3). In the Book of Acts, supernatural gifts attracted many new people to the Lord. (See, for example, Acts 3:11; 4:4, 33; 5:1-16.)

Thus, in furthering the ultimate purpose of glorifying Jesus as Lord, *the immediate purpose of the supernatural gifts is to edify, or build up, the church.* By building up the church, they glorify Christ, because the church is the body of Christ on earth. This building process occurs both by *adding new believers and strengthening existing believers.*

NOT PURPOSES

From this discussion and a study of the New Testament as a whole, we can also draw several conclusions about what the supernatural gifts are *not* meant to do.

This building process occurs both by adding new believers and strengthening existing believers.

The supernatural gifts do not replace the written Word of God. They do not supersede the authority of the Bible; they cannot alter its message. The Bible is our authority for instruction in salvation and Christian living. It is both necessary and sufficient for that purpose. "The Holy Scriptures . . . are able to make you wise for salvation through faith which is in Christ Jesus. All Scripture is given by inspiration of God, and is profitable for doctrine, for reproof, for correction, for instruction in righteousness, that the man of God may be complete, thoroughly equipped for every good work" (II Timothy 3:15-17).

The Bible is the eternal Word of God; He inspired it for all people everywhere. God will not tell an individual anything contrary to the written Word He has inspired for everyone. He gave the Bible for doctrinal instruction, and He would not thwart His own plan and purpose by bestowing gifts that would undermine the Bible's authority.

Clearly, then, the purpose of the spiritual gifts is not to teach doctrine. Their function is not to reveal the plan of salvation or principles of Christian living, although they can provide powerful confirmation of what the Bible teaches.

Consequently, we should beware when someone tries to use spiritual gifts as authority for doctrine or instruction in how a person should live. According to John 16:13, the manifested Spirit, or the Spirit within believers, does not grant independent authority to them but illuminates what God has already revealed and what Jesus taught on earth.

The purpose of the spiritual gifts is not to teach doctrine.

As an example, I Corinthians 14:29 says, "Let two or three prophets speak, and let the others judge." The listeners are to evaluate the apparent exercise of a spiritual gift, which means they must have an objective standard by which to do so. This authoritative standard is the gospel that the apostles preached. "But even if we, or an angel from heaven, preach any other gospel to you than what we have preached to you, let him be accursed" (Galatians 1:8). And this gospel has been communicated

47

to us by the written Word.

To illustrate, the Mormons claim that an angel named Moroni appeared to Joseph Smith and revealed the Book of Mormon to him, but according to Galatians, even if an angel did appear to Smith he had no authority to proclaim any doctrine other than what the Bible records. No other book can claim authority equal or similar to that of the Bible. (For further discussion, see *God's Infallible Word* by David K. Bernard.)

The Mormons also say that the Father and the Son appeared to Joseph Smith in a vision as two separate, visible persons of God. In Scripture, however, when the apostle Philip asked to see the Father, Jesus answered that the way to see the Father is to behold Jesus (John 14:9-11), for Jesus is the visible manifestation of the Father in flesh (Colossians 1:15, 19; 2:9; I Timothy 3:16). No miracle, vision, or other supernatural experience can change the truth of Scripture.

The supernatural gifts do not replace spiritual leadership in the church. Specifically, they do not supersede the authority of the pastor. As chapter 1 has discussed, God has given the fivefold ministry to the church for the equipping of the saints, and He has given pastors to lead, feed, and oversee the flock. God would not undermine the leaders He has appointed by prompting someone to challenge their authority.

God is not the author of confusion; He is the author of peace (I Corinthians 14:33). If someone announces, "Thus says the Lord, I rebuke the pastor," then the speaker is out of order, for God would not contradict His own principles of authority. He does not give spiritual gifts in such a way as to cause confusion, division, or rebellion.

If a pastor needs correction, God can speak to him directly. God can also use an individual with the right attitude and motives to discuss matters of concern with him in private. Serious problems can be referred to spiritual leaders who have the authority to deal with the situation scripturally so as to help both pastor and church.

Each Christian must learn to walk by faith, to grow in spiritual wisdom and knowledge, and to develop an understanding of God's will.

The supernatural gifts do not replace the daily guidance from God that we receive through prayer and submission of heart, mind, and will to Him. Each Christian must learn to walk by faith, to grow in spiritual wisdom and knowledge, and to develop an understanding of God's will. (See Colossians 1:9-11; 4:12.) Supernatural experiences do not provide a shortcut to spiritual maturity. We should not expect the supernatural gifts to be the primary means of determining God's will for our lives or the lives of others apart from prayer, the Word of God, and spiritual counsel.

Supernatural gifts can help to open our mind and heart to God's will, and they can help to confirm God's will. Thus through a gift of the Spirit, God revealed to the leadership of the church in Antioch the missionary calling of Barnabas and Paul: "The Holy Spirit said, 'Now separate to Me Barnabas and Saul for the work to which I have called them'" (Acts 13:2). Evidently God had already called these two men to this work. The spiritual utterance confirmed God's will to them and revealed it to the church, so that the church would send them with prayer and financial support.

We must find God's will for our lives through faithful prayer, Bible study, church attendance, godly leadership and counsel, and rational, practical consideration of the factors relevant to our decisions. Spiritual gifts can be part of this process but do not replace this process. Thus we should not heed someone who proclaims, "Thus says the Lord, you are to marry so-and-so," or even worse, "You are to divorce your companion and marry so-and-so." Both statements reflect a fundamental misunderstanding of how God works, and the second expressly contradicts Scripture. When God leads people, He respects their human personality and will; He does not coerce or manipulate. Moreover, when people sincerely seek Him, He answers their prayers and He guides them by various ways so that they can understand His will and have peace and assurance about it. While God sometimes speaks to us through miraculous events and utterances from others, if we have a relationship with Him we find that these various means work together and support one another, confirming what God speaks directly to our heart.

Summary

God bestows the supernatural gifts of the Spirit *to glorify Jesus Christ, to draw unbelievers to Him, and to strengthen and encourage believers.* They edify (build up) the body of Christ, His church. God does not give them to individuals as the means of teaching doctrine, superseding the fivefold ministry, or dictating His will for others' lives.

> *Those who attempt to exercise a spiritual gift outside these scriptural purposes are in error.*

Those who attempt to exercise a spiritual gift outside these scriptural purposes are in error. So are those who claim special authority because of a spiritual gift. The gift may be genuine but misunderstood or misused. Or the manifestation may be counterfeit—of the flesh or of the devil. Some of those who try to exercise spiritual gifts inappropriately may simply be ignorant, while others are carnal or even demonic. Some may manipulate for selfish motives; some may be deceitful or malicious.

In such cases, it is not imperative to offer a complete explanation of the underlying causes and motives of a certain manifestation. We can simply recognize that it is not in accordance with the Word of God and refuse to follow it. We can avoid the danger of false manifestations and improper uses by emphasizing the true purpose of the spiritual gifts. We are safe when we realize that God does not give them as a new source of authority in our lives, but for our edification, exhortation, and comfort.

CHAPTER FOUR

THE EXERCISE OF SPIRITUAL GIFTS

A s chapter 3 has discussed, it is important to exercise the gifts of the Spirit in accordance with God's purpose for granting them. A number of other issues are also important in considering their use.

AVAILABILITY OF SPIRITUAL GIFTS

"To the church of God which is at Corinth, to those who are sanctified in Christ Jesus, called to be saints, with all who in every place call on the name of Jesus Christ our Lord, both theirs and ours. . . . You were enriched in everything by Him in all utterance and all knowledge, even as the testimony of Christ was confirmed in you, so that you come short in no gift, eagerly waiting for the revelation of our Lord Jesus Christ" (I Corinthians 1:2, 5-7).

First, we must understand the availability of the spiritual gifts. Simply put, God has given them to the church. They are intended for every local body of believers until the return of the Lord Jesus Christ for His bride.

According to I Corinthians 1:2, Paul wrote this epistle not only to the church of Jesus Christ at Corinth but also to "all who in every place call on the name of Jesus Christ our Lord, both theirs and ours." These words describe every local body of believers without limits of space or time. Moreover, verse 7 affirms that the readers are to possess all the spiritual gifts until the Second Coming. Clearly, then, the discussion of spiritual gifts in I Corinthians 12-14 applies to every Christian congregation from apostolic times to the end of the present age.

Some people, such as traditional Protestants, believe that supernatural gifts ceased with the apostles or shortly thereafter. The Reformers Martin Luther and John Calvin held this view. Others, such as Roman Catholics, believe that miracles still occur but do not generally expect them in a local church setting.

Even charismatics typically do not expect the church as a whole to experience these gifts. For instance, at an international charismatic conference in 1991 in Brighton, England, a Roman Catholic priest argued that the entire Roman Catholic Church is charismatic (characterized by spiritual gifts), even though the vast majority of local churches and members never experience them. He reasoned as follows: Some people in the church speak in tongues and exercise other supernatural gifts; the church is united as one body; therefore the church is charismatic.

He considered this situation satisfactory and exemplary.

In contrast to these views, I Corinthians depicts every local body of believers as filled with the Spirit and experiencing supernatural gifts. The scriptural purpose and need for spiritual gifts did not end with the apostolic age, nor can we restrict the purpose and need for them to certain locations. While the church is universal, every local extension of the church should seek and expect the operation of supernatural gifts for as long as the church is in this world.

When the Lord returns for His church, there will be no further purpose for the gifts of the Spirit. We will not need miracles and healing because in the resurrection we will have glorified, immortal bodies. We will not need the word of wisdom and the word of knowledge because in eternity we will possess the fullness of divine wisdom and knowledge. Until then, however, we need the gifts of the Spirit.

Everyone who is filled with the Spirit can potentially operate any of the gifts.

Everyone who is filled with the Spirit can potentially operate any of the gifts, because they come from the Spirit. Not every individual will operate every gift, for the Spirit "distribut[es] to each one individually as He wills" (I Corinthians 12:11), but every congregation needs to actualize the potential for the gifts. Not everyone will prophesy or speak in tongues to the whole congregation, for instance, but every Spirit-filled person has the potential for doing so. (See I Corinthians 14:31.) Each individual should be open to any manifestation that God chooses.

DESIRING SPIRITUAL GIFTS

"Earnestly desire the best gifts. . . . Desire spiritual gifts" (I Corinthians 12:31; 14:1).

We should actively desire and seek all the gifts of the Spirit. While I Corinthians 12:31 speaks of "the best gifts," it does not identify which gifts are the best. Some may suppose that only a few of the nine gifts are superior and therefore desirable, but would God present us with a list of nine gifts and then tell us to seek only a few of them? Would the Spirit grant some gifts that are not desirable? In the only indication that a specific gift is better than another, I Corinthians 14 describes prophecy as superior to tongues in public meetings. It also underscores the value of tongues in private devotion, however, and it discloses that tongues is equal to prophecy in public meetings when there is an interpretation.

From this treatment, it appears that the "best" gift can vary depending on the circumstances. The best gift is the one most appropriate and needed at the moment. To desire the best gifts, then, is to seek whatever gifts are most important for our church at the time and to pray for the Lord to bestow them according to His perfect knowledge of our situation.

> *Christians should be sensitive to the leading of God's Spirit so that they are available for any manifestation God chooses.*

Christians should be sensitive to the leading of God's Spirit so that they are available for any manifestation God chooses. They should not limit their thinking to what they have experienced or observed in the past, but each of them should be open to "the best gifts" for the occasion.

As an example, if corporate worship reaches a holy pause in which the Spirit seeks to communicate with the congregation in a special way, each member should yield himself to God, realizing that, although God will not use everyone at that time, He wants to use someone. If a person speaks to the church in tongues, everyone should pray for the interpretation, anticipating that perhaps God would use him or her.

In the course of counseling, a pastor may reach an impasse in which no solution seems possible. He should pray and have faith for a word of wisdom or a word of knowledge. Perhaps serious trouble or confusion arises in the congregation, but the cause is unclear. The pastor should seek God for the discerning of spirits.

As needs arise and as God impresses us, we can

believe and pray for specific gifts. When we yield to the Spirit, God will work through us as He sees fit. If He chooses not to act miraculously at a given time, we continue to walk by faith, recognizing that God knows things we do not and makes plans beyond our understanding. Given His perfect knowledge of the situation, He may choose not to act as we expect, due to attitudes or circumstances we cannot see. He may use someone else, or He may work in a different way altogether. In some cases a lack of faith or surrender on our part may hinder His work, and we must learn to be more responsive in the future.

GIFTS ARE NOT A SIGN OF SPIRITUAL MATURITY

"Men of Israel, why do you marvel at this? Or why look so intently at us, as though by our own power or godliness we had made this man walk?" (Acts 3:12).

While we must desire spiritual gifts and learn to open our lives to them, we must realize that, in itself, the exercise of spiritual gifts is not necessarily a sign of spiritual maturity. This concept surprises many people because they wrongly assume that if God uses a person in a miraculous way then the person must be extraordinarily spiritual.

The spiritual gifts, however, are truly gifts: they come freely, by God's grace. As we have seen, the Greek word for "gift" in I Corinthians 12 is *charisma*, which is closely related to *charis*, the word for "grace." By definition, a gift is not something that a person has purchased or earned.

The quality of a gift reveals little or nothing about the recipient, but it can indicate much about the giver. If a gift is expensive and elaborate, the recipient could be rich or poor, deserving or undeserving, of noble or ignoble character. What we learn from such a gift is that the giver has substantial resources, is generous, and is greatly interested in the recipient.

An awesome display of spiritual gifts should remind us of how powerful and gracious God is.

So it is with the spiritual gifts. An awesome display of spiritual gifts should remind us of how powerful and gracious God is. We should not focus on the individual who receives the gift, concluding that he is a great prophet or the most spiritual person in church. Of course, it is evident that he has faith for the gift and has learned to yield to God's Spirit. We can appreciate his sensitivity in this area, but he may or may not have the same degree of faith and surrender in other areas of his life.

According to Jesus, some people will have faith to prophesy, cast out demons, and do wonderful works in His name, yet because of their disobedience to the will of God they will not enter into the kingdom of heaven. (See

Matthew 7:21-27.) It is possible, then, for someone to receive and exercise a spiritual gift yet adhere to a false doctrine or participate in a sinful practice.

In Acts 3, multitudes of people gathered around Peter and John in response to the healing of a lame man. Peter admonished them not to think this miracle occurred because of the apostles' own power or holiness but pointed the people to Jesus. In other words, the miracle did not indicate that Peter and John were more spiritual than someone else. They prayed in the name of Jesus, exercising faith in Him, and He performed the work.

The same principle is true with respect to expressions of worship. If someone dances in the Spirit or falls prostrate on the floor under the power of God, we learn nothing about his spiritual status. Often the most spiritual persons worship the most freely. On the other hand, sometimes the most carnal persons worship freely as well, enjoying the emotional experience, the attention of others, or both. Sometimes notoriously inconsistent people receive dramatic blessings in worship; perhaps God blesses them so greatly because that is what they need to stay in church or because it takes extraordinary measures to draw them close to Him. In such cases, we simply acknowledge the greatness of God's mercy and grace.

In short, when we see a notable spiritual manifestation, we recognize that the individual has yielded to God at this point. He has learned to be sensitive to the Spirit, to surrender his will, to lay aside his inhibitions, to take God at His Word, and to have faith for God to bless him. These qualities are admirable, and when applied to all areas of life, they will result in spiritual maturity.

We cannot draw any further conclusions about the individual's life or doctrine, however. He may be spiritually mature or immature. A spiritual gift or manifestation is no sign of spiritual maturity, nor is it an endorsement of the total person. The gift simply reveals how great God is.

A spiritual gift or manifestation is no sign of spiritual maturity, but simply reveals how great God is.

Understanding this principle will lead to a greater exercise of spiritual gifts. When people stop focusing on their inability and lack of qualifications and instead focus on the grace and power of God, it becomes easier for them to have faith for spiritual gifts. Moreover, perhaps God limits or withholds some gifts in certain situations because of people who are prone to misunderstand them or exaggerate their significance. Since the Spirit always exalts Jesus, there will be greater freedom and manifestations of the Spirit when people do not allow spiritual gifts to result in pride, hero worship, or endorsement of false doctrine or lifestyle.

YIELDED TO THE SPIRIT

"And His name, through faith in His name, has made this man strong, whom you see and know. Yes,

the faith which comes through Him has given him this perfect soundness in the presence of you all" (Acts 3:16).

"Do not quench the Spirit" (I Thessalonians 5:19).

As Peter explained about the healing of the lame man, the key to exercising spiritual gifts is *faith in Jesus Christ*. In its fullest sense, faith means trust in the Lord and reliance upon Him. Instead of depending upon our abilities, we must depend on God's. Instead of boasting of our qualifications or accomplishments, we must boast about the death, burial, and resurrection of Jesus Christ. Instead of developing clever, intricate strategies for spiritual achievement, we must appropriate the victory Jesus has already won for us. Instead of trusting in our background, knowledge, or experience, we must rely upon the work of the Holy Spirit, the Spirit of the risen Lord. Instead of quenching the Spirit, we must yield to the Spirit.

Humility is vital in the exercise of all spiritual gifts and abilities.

Relying on the Holy Spirit requires *humility, brokenness, and yieldedness*. Humility is vital in the exercise of all spiritual gifts and abilities. (See Romans 12:3-6.) "Yes, all of you be submissive to one another, and be clothed with humility, for 'God resists the proud, but gives grace to the humble.' Therefore humble yourselves under the mighty hand of God, that He may exalt you in due time" (I Peter 5:5-6). "The LORD is near to those who have a broken heart, and saves such as have a contrite spirit" (Psalm 34:18). "I beseech you therefore, brethren, by the mercies of God, that you present your bodies a living sacrifice, holy, acceptable to God, which is your reasonable service" (Romans 12:1).

Humility, brokenness, and yieldedness are important in all aspects of Christian life, but these attributes are particularly vital in allowing God's Spirit to work through us. We should be neither proud nor self-rejecting, but simply unconscious of self. We need a hunger for the things of God and a sincere love for the kingdom of God. We must repent of sin and pursue holiness, asking the Lord to reveal and remove secret impurities in our life. We should periodically evaluate and purge our motives. We should develop a habit of prayer and a continual attitude of prayer. Self-discipline and self-denial should become guiding principles of our life, and fasting is an important practice in this regard.

We cannot earn favors from God through spiritual efforts, but these attitudes and disciplines will help minimize worldly influences and maximize godly influences. As we lay aside selfish desires and fleshly lusts, we will become more sensitive and open to the things of God.

Learning to walk by faith and to yield to the Spirit is a process. We grow in grace and knowledge (II Peter 3:18). It is not difficult to allow God to work through us, but it does take mental, emotional, and spiritual adjustments. We must lay aside fear and doubt and let the Spirit flow through us.

The same principles are at work as when we first received the Holy Spirit and spoke in tongues. The gift of the Holy Spirit comes by grace through faith, and after people receive it they invariably acknowledge how simple it is to receive. Some pray many times and for many hours, however, before being baptized with the Holy Spirit—not because the experience itself is difficult to receive but because they must fully repent; learn to put away guilt, fear, and doubt; accept the gift by an active, present faith; and yield their mind and body to God's control.

When God first begins to use people in a certain way, they are often nervous, hesitant, or fearful—afraid of the unknown, afraid of rejection, afraid of being out of order. When they overcome these feelings and act in faith, then the Spirit flows freely through them. Often they need just a little confirmation or encouragement to surrender completely.

When they act in faith, then the Spirit flows freely through them.

In the early part of my marriage and ministry, I was leading a service when someone spoke to the congregation in tongues. I felt that God would give the interpretation to my wife, so I walked over to her and placed my hand on her. Immediately she began giving the interpretation. She had felt God moving upon her, but this experience was new to her, and she was hesitant to respond. My action gave her the confirmation she needed.

In another service, I observed a similar incident. As God moved in a special way, the emcee walked over to a young minister, recognizing that God wanted to speak through him, and laid his hands on his shoulder. Immediately the young man began to prophesy.

When my wife and I started a church in Austin, Texas, we began with services in our house. Soon we were able to share a building with another church for two services a week, but we continued to hold prayer meetings at home. While we were still small, I began to teach on the gifts of the Spirit and tell the people that God wanted these gifts to operate in our group. In one prayer meeting, as the Lord moved greatly, I realized that God wanted to speak through my wife's grandmother. Although she was in her seventies and had been raised in the Pentecostal movement, she had never been used in this way before, and she was hesitant to yield.

Afterwards, I told her, "Grannie, you have always been in churches where there were many people who knew how to respond to God, but now you are in a young church in which most of the people have not had much experience. We need people like you who know how to respond to God. So the next time you feel what you did tonight, go ahead and let God speak through you." Not long afterwards, in another prayer meeting, she did yield, speaking to the group in tongues, and an interpretation followed.

It is possible for a person to operate a certain gift only once, but typically people will operate the same gift repeatedly. Once they overcome their initial hesitation, step out by faith, and surrender themselves to God, it is much easier for God to use them again in the same way. Nevertheless, we should not allow ourselves to get into a rut either as individuals or as churches. If we have been used in a certain way before, we should not automatically assume that God will use us instead of someone else the next time. Likewise, if God has frequently used another church member in a certain way, we should not assume that he is the only one God wants to use in that way. Instead, each time God moves and each time a need arises, all of us should seek after God and be sensitive to His will and His work at that moment.

OPERATING THE GIFTS IN LOVE

"Though I speak with the tongues of men and of angels, but have not love, I have become as sounding brass or a clanging cymbal. And though I have the gift of prophecy, and understand all mysteries and all knowledge, and though I have all faith, so that I could remove mountains, but have not love, I am nothing. . . . Pursue love, and desire spiritual gifts" (I Corinthians 13:1-2; 14:1).

The most important thing we can say about the exercise of spiritual gifts is that we must operate them in love. In the middle of the discussion of supernatural gifts

66

in I Corinthians 12-14, one entire chapter—I Corinthians 13—is devoted to the subject of love. One of the most beautiful passages of Scripture, it is often quoted for its teachings on love in general, and rightly so. Yet we should not forget that its most immediate application is in the context of spiritual gifts.

The gifts have no value unless they are operated in love.

The chapter emphatically states that the gifts have no value unless they are operated in love. It is not God's will for someone to attempt to use a spiritual gift in a harsh, destructive, condemning, manipulative, intimidating, or disruptive way.

Such manifestations are either completely false or, at the least, abuses of what God is seeking to accomplish. The only proper way to exercise spiritual gifts is with a heart filled with love for God and love for one another. (See chapter 6 for further discussion of love.)

Here are some examples that violate the principle of love. In one church that was experiencing conflict, a person gave a public message alleging that a certain disgruntled individual would try to kill members of the pastor's family. In another case, a pastor learned that a family in his church was contemplating an action of which he disapproved. He told them that God had spoken to him about the matter and implied that if they acted contrary to the pastor's wish then death might visit the family. In a third situation, a church member began giving private prophecies of doom to others in the church, telling one person in poor health that this individual would soon die but without offering any constructive reason why God would disclose such information.

In each case, there was an alleged use of a spiritual gift, but not for the purpose of edification, exhortation, and comfort and not as an expression of love for others. Even if some of the statements contained an element of truth, they were not made in a redemptive, constructive way with respect and love for everyone involved. Instead, these actions only damaged individuals or congregations.

THE GIFTS ARE SUBJECT TO THE RECIPIENT'S CONTROL

"And the spirits of the prophets are subject to the prophets. For God is not the author of confusion but of peace, as in all the churches of the saints. . . . Let all things be done decently and in order" (I Corinthians 14:32-33, 40).

The gifts of the Spirit are subject to the control of the user.

The gifts of the Spirit are subject to the control of the user. When God gives gifts, He does not override the human will. We still retain the choice to use God's gifts properly or improperly, and He expects us to use them appropriately. This principle holds true for all the blessings of God, including life itself, health, material possessions, finances, talents, abilities, ministries, positions of leadership, and supernatural gifts.

Some people assume that because the gifts of the Spirit are supernatural, the recipients have little or no control over them. They think God overwhelms recipients so that they act almost unconsciously, in a trancelike or robotic state. But God always respects the human personality and will, for he created us in His image as intelligent, rational, moral beings with the power of choice. In all manifestations, the recipients must yield to God, but God still allows them to retain a degree of control. As an inevitable consequence of this freedom of choice, there is always the potential for abuse or misuse.

As an Old Testament example, God gave Moses power to bring forth water out of a rock for Israel. On one occasion God told Moses to speak to the rock. Instead, Moses struck the rock in anger at the rebelliousness of Israel. Since Moses disobeyed God in this matter, God did not let him enter the Promised Land. (See Numbers 20:7-12.)

Because of the possibility of misuse I Corinthians 14:32 says, "And the spirits of the prophets are subject to the prophets." Humans cannot control or dictate to the Spirit of God, but the Spirit works through human spirits, and humans exercise control over their own spirits. God retains ultimate control over the bestowal of spiritual gifts, but He gives humans great freedom regarding their use. While we cannot determine who will receive what gifts, and while we should not try to force certain gifts to operate when, where, and how we desire, we do have a personal responsibility to use the gifts as God has intended—for His glory, for edification of the body, and with love for all concerned.

> *We do have a personal responsibility to use the gifts as God has intended.*

Speaking in tongues is a good example. It comes as the Spirit gives utterance (Acts 2:4), not by human learning or imitation of sounds. When someone first receives the Holy Spirit, he will speak in tongues as the initial sign, and in most cases he will continue to speak in tongues from time to time in his private devotional life. As he grows in the Lord, he can learn to yield to God and pray earnestly so that he will speak in tongues often. While the utterance continues to come from God, the individual can create conditions conducive to speaking in tongues, and therefore he has a responsibility to exercise this gift appropriately.

In my case, I do not speak in tongues every time I pray, but when I am in deep, intercessory prayer I often begin to speak in tongues without conscious forethought. At almost any place and time, then, I could pray earnestly until I spoke in tongues, and I could pray as loudly as I wished. Under normal circumstances, however, it would not be appropriate for me to kneel in the aisle of a super-market, in the middle of a highway, or in a public school classroom and pray until I spoke in tongues loudly. If I did, the Spirit would enable me to speak in tongues, not the flesh or the devil, yet the time and place would be inappropriate. Instead of glorifying the Lord, attracting sinners to Him, and building up saints, such a use would be a hindrance, distraction, and reproach.

Some say God would stop any misuse of a gift. Some cite abuses as evidence that all claimed spiritual manifes-tations are false, and some use abuses to advocate that we should not seek any supernatural manifestations. But the antidote to misuse and abuse is not disuse but proper use. Moreover, such people simply do not understand how God operates. He responds to faith wherever He finds it, He fulfills His Word to everyone who invokes it, and when He grants a gift He also gives the authority and responsi-bility to use that gift.

Jesus taught, "Do not give what is holy to the dogs; nor cast your pearls before swine" (Matthew 7:6). He thereby indicated that some uses of holy blessings and spiritual gifts are unprofitable, unsuitable, or detrimental. Paul wrote of the nation of Israel, "For the gifts and the calling of God are irrevocable" (Romans 11:29). Even though Israel as a nation failed to fulfill God's purpose, God continued to work in their midst to redirect them back into His plan.

Thus a person can have faith for a genuine miracle from God but then misuse that miracle to promote self, to endorse false doctrine, to seek worldly fame, or to profit materially. An example is the healing of Naaman from leprosy through the ministry of Elisha. Elisha refused Naaman's offer of payment, but Elisha's servant, Gehazi, later took money and clothing from Naaman and thereby incurred divine judgment. (See II Kings 5.)

God's purpose in granting a miracle is always good.

We must not fault God for such abuses and the resulting confusion. God's purpose in granting a miracle is always good. In every case He acts out of grace, responds to faith, fulfills His Word, and meets genuine needs. It is our responsibility to use these gifts according to the guidelines He has given us. It is also our responsibility to judge all manifestations to see whether they are of God and, even if they are, to see whether they are used appropriately. (See I Corinthians 14:29, 37; I John 4:1.) Mature Christians can recognize a genuine move of God. They can also acknowledge a genuine manifestation without accepting a mistaken interpretation or use of it. For instance, they can recognize a divine healing but reject a claim of extrabiblical authority by the person who prayed for the healing.

Some manifestations are fleshly, demonic, or fake, but sometimes a genuine spiritual work is used inappropriately. For instance, let us suppose God grants a word of knowledge to a pastor about a serious sin in the church he leads. God's purpose is to protect the pastor and church and to restore the sinner. Depending on the circumstances, the best use of this knowledge may be for the pastor to counsel privately with the wrongdoer, to act behind the scenes to minimize damage, to confidentially warn another individual who is affected, or simply to pray and be cautious until a later time. If the pastor announces the secret sin to the entire congregation, however, he would probably misuse the word of knowledge, for this action would likely harm everyone involved without accomplishing God's purpose.

Some people say that when they feel the Spirit, they should act without restraint and any guidelines would quench the Spirit. In opposition to this view, under divine inspiration Paul wrote, "If anyone thinks himself to be a prophet or spiritual, let him acknowledge that the things which I write to you are the commandments of the Lord. But if anyone is ignorant, let him be ignorant" (I Corinthians 14:37-38).

Those who are truly spiritual will acknowledge the need for biblical guidelines, not because they do not trust the Spirit but because they do not trust the flesh. Instead of depending solely on subjective feelings and impressions, they are guided foremost by the objective principles and instructions of God's Word, realizing that the Spirit who moves upon them has already established universal guidelines to govern His gifts. To think otherwise is a mark of ignorance.

We can summarize much of our discussion by the following admonition: "Let all things be done decently and in order" (I Corinthians 14:40). In every exercise of a spiritual gift we should support church unity and spiritual leadership. In every worship service we should seek the maximum benefit of everyone present, believers and unbelievers alike.

"Let all things be done decently and in order."

Let us suppose someone captures everyone's attention in a public service by speaking loudly in tongues. Typically the pastor or worship leader will pause to allow the operation of tongues and interpretation. But what if the leader continues on with the order of the service or makes a deliberate transition to another part of the service? The congregation should follow this direction. They would not be quenching the Spirit; they would be doing all things decently and in order.

There are several possible explanations of this situation, but regardless of which one is correct, the church still needs to follow the spiritual leader, for it is his God-given responsibility to direct the overall service. First, the individual who spoke in tongues may simply have received a personal blessing; the particular work of the Spirit may have been for him alone. The leader, however, sensed the direction of the Lord for the whole congregation and acted accordingly.

Second, the individual may have acted out of a mistaken feeling, excessive zeal, carnality, or even demonic influence. In such a case, the leader had a responsibility to protect the congregation, and everyone had a responsibility to cooperate with the leader.

Third, it is possible that the leader missed the direction of the Spirit. In such a case, however, an individual will do more harm than good by trying to push the service contrary to the leader. The result will be confusion and division.

Most likely, the person in spiritual leadership will make the correct decision, but even if he does not, the best way to handle the situation is to cooperate and promote unity. God can easily accomplish His purpose in another way or move upon the leader at a later time, and a momentary mistake need not cause any lasting harm. The damage caused by indecent or disorderly conduct, however, is often permanent.

In sum, each congregation and each Christian should earnestly seek the gifts of the Spirit. At the same time, all of us must learn to exercise the gifts according to scriptural principles—lovingly, decently, and in divine order.

CHAPTER FIVE

I CORINTHIANS 12: SPIRITUAL GIFTS IN THE BODY OF CHRIST

In the whole of Scripture, I Corinthians 12-14 provides the most extended discussion of the supernatural gifts of the Spirit. I Corinthians 12:1-11 introduces and identifies these gifts, while I Corinthians 12:12-31 describes how the church functions as the body of Christ with individual members exercising a diversity of gifts. I Corinthians 13 teaches the supremacy of love in the operation of spiritual gifts. Then I Corinthians 14 provides guidelines for the vocal gifts—prophecy, tongues, and interpretation of tongues. Before examining each of the nine supernatural gifts, including the vocal gifts, it is helpful to analyze the teaching of I Corinthians 12-13, which serves as a foundation for further study.

INTRODUCTION TO SPIRITUAL GIFTS (I CORINTHIANS 12:1-11)

"Now concerning spiritual gifts, brethren, I do not want you to be ignorant: you know that you were

Gentiles, carried away to these dumb idols, however you were led" (verses 1-2).

The Corinthian church emerged out of a pagan Gentile background. Before they came to Jesus Christ, they had no knowledge of the work of the Holy Spirit, but they were completely led astray in spiritual matters by their idolatrous worship. Consequently, the apostle Paul, under divine inspiration, felt it necessary to teach them about spiritual gifts.

The Corinthian believers had already been baptized in the name of Jesus Christ and baptized with the Holy Spirit. (See I Corinthians 1:13; 6:11; 12:13.) Their new-found faith and spiritual rebirth did not automatically impart mature knowledge of spiritual matters, however. They needed instruction and guidance in this area, and so do Christians today.

"Therefore I make known to you that no one speaking by the Spirit of God calls Jesus accursed, and no one can say that Jesus is Lord except by the Holy Spirit" (verse 3).

Because of their lack of previous spiritual knowledge and experience, the Corinthians were vulnerable to false manifestations. Therefore, a simple test would help them distinguish the genuine from the false: If someone denounces Jesus Christ, he cannot be of God. If a spirit does not exalt the Lord Jesus Christ—no matter how miraculous, spectacular, or beguiling it may be—then it is not of God. After all, the purpose of the Holy Spirit is to glorify Jesus (John 16:14).

This test is similar to the ones recorded in the Old Testament, with the added recognition that Jesus Christ is God manifested in flesh, our Lord and God. (See John 20:28; I Timothy 3:16.) God told His people to reject any dreamer or miracle worker who tried to lead them to worship other gods and to reject any prophet who spoke in the name of other gods (Deuteronomy 13:1-3; 18:20).

Not only will the Spirit never lead someone to curse or blaspheme Jesus, but no one can truly say that Jesus is Lord except by the Holy Spirit. Whenever someone truly understands who Jesus is, and whenever someone truly submits his life to Jesus, we should acknowledge it as the work of the Holy Spirit.

This statement is not strictly part of the test, for the purpose of the test is to tell when something is *not* of God, but it simply expresses a corollary. It does not mean that everyone who makes a verbal confession of Jesus is full of the Holy Spirit, lives a godly life, or is saved. Nor does it mean that every act or pronouncement of such a person is the work of the Spirit. There is often a gap between profession and reality, between mental acknowledgment and saving faith, between verbal confession and obedience. (See Matthew 7:21-27; Luke 13:24-30; John 2:23-25; 12:42-43; James 2:19-20.)

Instead, the second half of verse 3 states that the grace of God, which appears to everyone, is the source of all true spiritual understanding and experience. (See Titus 2:11; 3:4-7.) It is God who leads a person to the point of confessing that Jesus is Lord. When Peter confessed that Jesus was the Christ (Messiah), the Son of the living God (God manifest in flesh), Jesus responded, "Flesh and blood has not revealed this to you, but My Father who is in heaven" (Matthew 16:16-17). Ultimately, no one can truly understand the identity of Jesus Christ, including the union of full deity and perfect humanity in Him, without the illumination of the Holy Spirit. The Scriptures declare this truth, but the Spirit of God must illuminate it to our hearts and minds. Human intellect, education, philosophy, and tradition are all inadequate for this task. (See Colossians 2:8-9.)

There is a further implication for Christian living, in that truly confessing Jesus as Lord involves actually making Him the Lord of our lives. (See Luke 6:46.) The only way we can make this confession an everyday reality is by the power of the Holy Spirit. The Holy Spirit enables us to turn from sin, begin a new life, bear witness in both word and deed of our changed life, produce spiritual fruit, and walk in holiness. (See Acts 1:8; Romans 8:13; Galatians 5:22-23.)

We should seek the unique work of God in our own lives.

"There are diversities of gifts, but the same Spirit. There are differences of ministries, but the same Lord. And there are diversities of activities, but it is

the same God who works all in all" (verses 4-6).

The Lord works in various ways, bestowing different gifts, ministries, and activities upon different individuals. But it is the same Spirit who grants all of them. We should all desire spiritual gifts, but we should not all expect to be used in the same way. We should not be envious of others, or seek to imitate them, but we should seek the unique work of God in our own lives.

Moreover, we should not judge people's spirituality by the kind of gifts they exercise. While some gifts are more prominent or visible than others, it is the same God who works in every member of the church.

This passage uses three titles of God to convey different nuances of meaning, but the overriding theme is the oneness of God and the oneness of His work in the church. The title "God" is the most general, referring to the totality of the divine essence and work. The title "Lord" means "master, ruler" and emphasizes God's decision-making authority and administrative power. The title "Spirit" describes the one God in supernatural action, particularly in our world and in individual lives. The Holy Spirit is not a separate entity from God, but "the Spirit of God," "the Spirit of Jesus Christ," and "the Spirit of your Father." (See Matthew 10:20; Philippians 1:19; Romans 8:9.)

"But the manifestation of the Spirit is given to each one for the profit of all: for to one is given the word of wisdom through the Spirit, to another the word of knowledge through the same Spirit, to another

faith by the same Spirit, to another gifts of healings by the same Spirit, to another the working of miracles, to another prophecy, to another discerning of spirits, to another different kinds of tongues, to another the interpretation of tongues. But one and the same Spirit works all these things, distributing to each one individually as He wills" (verses 7-11).

As we discussed in chapter 2, God is the source of the gifts, and He grants them according to His will. Any doctrine or practice that promotes the allocation or exercise of spiritual gifts according to human desires and schemes is erroneous.

The passage repeatedly states that each gift comes by "the same Spirit," echoing verses 4-6. That people receive different gifts is no basis for pride, competition, disunity, or strife, because all gifts come by "one and the same Spirit" (verse 11).

God grants the gifts for the benefit of everyone.

As chapter 3 has discussed, God grants the gifts for the benefit of everyone. While the manifestations come to individuals, the purpose is to build up the body.

In this connection, a question arises as to whether the gifts belong to individuals or to the church. If someone gives a prophecy, should we say he holds the office of prophet? Should we say he permanently possesses the gift of prophecy, or should we simply say he has exercised the gift of prophecy on a particular occasion? If someone prays for several sick people and they are immediately cured, should we identify him as a healer? Does he have a resident gift of healing, and if so, should we consistently bring the sick to him for prayer? Would there be any value in asking someone to pray for the sick if he does *not* claim this gift, or should we take them exclusively to a recognized "healer"? Is it appropriate to advertise, as one self-proclaimed "apostle" did of himself in a charismatic magazine, that someone possesses all nine gifts of the Spirit?

To answer these questions, we must reconcile two strands of scriptural thought. On the one hand, verses 8-10 state that God gives distinct gifts to specific individuals: one gift is given "to one," and a different gift is given "to another." Verses 29-30 indicate that some people, but not all, are "workers of miracles" and "have gifts of healing."

On the other hand, the overall theme of I Corinthians 12 is that God gives the gifts "for the profit of all" (verse 7) and to operate within the "one body" (verse 13). Just as the foot or ear cannot function in isolation from the rest of the body, so the members of the church cannot function apart from the rest of the church (verses 15-25).

Jesus promised miracles and healing to all believers, not just to a select few: "And these signs will follow those who believe: In My name they will cast out demons; they will speak with new tongues; they will take up serpents; and if they drink anything deadly, it will by no means hurt them; they will lay hands on the sick, and they will recover" (Mark 16:17-18). Similarly, all the elders of the church, not just certain "healers," are qualified to pray for the sick to be healed: "Is anyone among you sick? Let him call for the elders of the church, and let them pray over him, anointing him with oil in the name of the Lord. And the prayer of faith will save the sick, and the Lord will raise him up" (James 5:14-15).

The Spirit grants supernatural gifts to the church for individuals to exercise.

Perhaps the best explanation is that *the Spirit grants supernatural gifts to the church for individuals to exercise*, as He wills and works and as the need arises. The gifts operate through individuals, but each manifestation is a gift to the body and not merely to the individual through whom it comes. A person often exercises the same gift repeatedly, not because he owns it but because he can easily have faith for it again and again. Every manifestation is as the "Spirit"—not the individual—"wills" and "works" in the church (I Corinthians 12:11).

Under this view, not everyone will exercise every gift, but each person can potentially exercise any gift. No gift is the exclusive possession of a select few. This understanding seems to be the only way to resolve two very different statements about the gift of prophecy: God enables only some people to prophesy (at least on a certain occasion), but He gives everyone permission to prophesy (as He moves). "There are diversities of gifts. . . . For to one is given the word of wisdom . . . to another prophecy" (I Corinthians 12:4, 8, 10). "You can all prophesy one by one" (I Corinthians 14:31).

Emphasizing the corporate possession of the gifts helps us to avoid spiritual pride and encourages us to remain dependent upon each other and the Holy Spirit. While it is proper to have confidence in and appreciation for individuals who frequently yield to God in the exercise of certain gifts, we should not depend upon them but upon the Spirit and the body as a whole. If we need a word of wisdom or a healing, and no one who has recognized experience in this gift is present, we can still unite in faith and trust God to meet the need.

In a corporate setting, we look to spiritual leaders, as when we ask the elders to pray for the sick in accordance with James 5:14-15. If an urgent need arises in our everyday life, however, or if a sudden opportunity arises as we witness to someone, we are not handicapped because a spiritual leader is not available. Since each believer is an extension of the church and its representative to the world around him, each of us can pray for instantaneous healing, divine protection, or some other miracle, as Mark 16:16-17 promises.

I Corinthians 12:8-10 lists nine supernatural gifts of the Spirit. For the sake of study, it is common to classify them under three headings, as follows:

A. Gifts of Revelation

1. Word of wisdom
2. Word of knowledge
3. Discerning of spirits

B. Gifts of Power

1. Faith
2. Working of miracles
3. Gifts of healings

C. Gifts of Utterance

1. Prophecy
2. Different kinds of tongues
3. Interpretation of tongues

Using the scriptural identification of the church as the body of Christ, which immediately follows the list of the nine gifts, we can also describe these three categories respectively as manifestations of *the mind of Christ, the hands of Christ, and the voice of Christ*. We will discuss these nine gifts individually in chapters 7-13.

EXERCISING SPIRITUAL GIFTS IN THE BODY
(I CORINTHIANS 12:12-31)

"For as the body is one and has many members, but all the members of that one body, being many, are one body, so also is Christ. For by one Spirit we were all baptized into one body—whether Jews or Greeks, whether slaves or free—and have all been made to

drink into one Spirit" (verses 12-13).

Immediately after listing the nine spiritual gifts, I Corinthians 12 describes the church as the body of Christ. The overriding theme is unity amid diversity. Regardless of our various ethnic and social backgrounds, the one Spirit of God makes us all one body in Christ, even as He uses us in unique ways.

The baptism of the Holy Spirit places us into the one body of Christ.

From verse 13 we see the importance of being baptized with the Holy Spirit. The baptism of the Holy Spirit places us into the one body of Christ. This statement does not deny the complementary role of water baptism but mentions only the Spirit because the theme of the passage is the work of the Spirit and because it is through the Spirit that we have living communion. (See II Corinthians 13:14; Philippians 2:1.) Other passages teach that water baptism in the name of Jesus Christ is also part of Christian initiation. (See Acts 2:37-41; Romans 6:3-4; I Corinthians 6:11; Galatians 3:27.) Here, Paul probably assumed the typical case of water baptism prior to Spirit baptism (Acts 2:38). He reminded his readers that, after water baptism, when they proceeded to receive the Holy Spirit they were plunged into living, spiritual fellowship with Christ and His church. Just as an empty vessel is filled when it is immersed, so they began to drink deeply of the Spirit as this overwhelming experience flooded them.

In Acts 1:5, Jesus promised the disciples, "You shall be baptized with the Holy Spirit not many days from now." The Greek preposition translated "with" here is *en*, which is also translated "by" or "in." Indeed, I Corinthians 12:13 uses the same Greek preposition to say that we have all been baptized "by" one Spirit. Linguistically, then, the promise of Jesus in Acts 1:5 and the description of Paul in I Corinthians 12:13 refer to the same event.

The promise of Jesus was fulfilled on the Day of Pentecost: "And they were all filled with the Holy Spirit and began to speak with other tongues, as the Spirit gave them utterance" (Acts 2:4). That day, Peter described this experience as the Spirit being "poured out" and as "receiv[ing] the gift of the Holy Spirit" (Acts 2:33, 38). When Gentiles later received the same experience, the Bible says "the Holy Spirit fell on" them, "the gift of the Holy Spirit [was] poured out" on them, and they "received the Holy Spirit" (Acts 10:44-47; 11:15-17).

Clearly, then, by the same supernatural experience the same Spirit incorporates us into the body of Christ and also gives us power to be living witnesses, power to produce spiritual fruit, and power to exercise spiritual gifts. (See Acts 1:8; I Corinthians 12:8-10; Galatians 5:22-23.) It is a mistake to differentiate sharply between receiving the Spirit to enter the body of Christ and receiving the Spirit for power to serve the body of Christ. We do not join the body as a nonfunctional member. We receive one Spirit (not two or three) in one comprehensive initiatory experience, and the one Spirit brings with Him the potential for all spiritual fruit and gifts.

"For in fact the body is not one member but many. If the foot should say, 'Because I am not a hand, I am not of the body,' is it therefore not of the body? And if the ear should say, 'Because I am not an eye, I am not of the body,' is it therefore not of the body? If the whole body were an eye, where would be the hearing? If the whole were hearing, where would be the smelling? But now God has set the members, each one of them, in the body just as He pleased. And if they were all one member, where would the body be? But now indeed there are many members, yet one body. And the eye cannot say to the hand, 'I have no need of you'; nor again the head to the feet, 'I have no need of you.' No, much rather, those members of the body which seem to be weaker are necessary. And those members of the body which we think to be less honorable, on these we bestow greater honor; and our unpresentable parts have greater modesty, but our presentable parts have no need. But God composed the body, having given greater honor to that part which lacks it, that there should be no schism in the body, but that the members should have the same care for one another. And if one member suffers, all the members suffer with it; or if one member is honored, all the members rejoice with it" (verses 14-26).

This passage elaborates on the description of the church as the body of Christ and stresses the theme of unity amid diversity. Because the spiritual gifts are so supernatural and spectacular, it is easy for pride, hero worship, jealousy, and contention to result from their use if we do not understand how the body of Christ works. The analogy to the human body teaches us several important lessons that enable us to exercise the gifts harmoniously and beneficially:

1. *The church is united but not uniform; there is unity amid diversity* (verses 14, 20).

2. *To function effectively, the members need unity and must acknowledge their role as part of the body* (verses 15-16).

3. *To function effectively, the church needs diversity and must acknowledge the various roles of its members* (verses 17, 19).

4. *God is the one who has ordained this unity amid diversity; He has designed our different roles as He sees fit* (verse 18).

5. *Every member is needed and valuable, even though some receive less recognition than others* (verses 21-24).

6. *The members should strive for unity, prevent divisions, and cultivate mutual care and respect* (verses 25-26).

If we do not understand these principles, we may think that because a person exercises a spectacular gift he is thereby more spiritual, more important, or more worthy than others in the church. And such a person may think that he does not need the fellowship, discipline, guidance, and spiritual leadership of the church. But when we study the operation of the human body, we find that the body needs all its members, and all the members need the body.

For instance, the parts of the body that seem to be weak and vulnerable, such as our internal organs, are actually indispensable. Some parts seem less honorable, valuable, or vital—like hair—yet we treat them with special honor. Our unpresentable parts we treat with special modesty, while our presentable parts, such as our hands, do not require such treatment. Some parts have greater visibility, others have greater utility, but all serve a purpose.

Each assembly needs the benefit of the full range of spiritual gifts, and each member needs to be an active part of the body.

So it is in the body of Christ. Each assembly needs the benefit of the full range of spiritual gifts, and each member needs to be an active part of the body.

"Now you are the body of Christ, and members individually. And God has appointed these in the church: first apostles, second prophets, third teachers, after that miracles, then gifts of healings, helps, administrations, varieties of tongues. Are all apostles?

Are all prophets? Are all teachers? Are all workers of miracles? Do all have gifts of healings? Do all speak with tongues? Do all interpret?" (verses 27-30).

This passage applies the body analogy to the discussion of spiritual gifts. As we noted in chapter 1, these verses provide examples of the ministerial office gifts (apostles, prophets, teachers), the service gifts (helps, administrations), and the supernatural spiritual gifts (miracles, healings, tongues, interpretation).

The order of the list indicates that the ministerial office gifts are the most important to the function of the church, followed by the supernatural gifts of power, then the service gifts, and finally the supernatural gifts of utterance. We must not make too much of this order or of the omission of some gifts here. The passage simply lists examples; its purpose is not to give a precise, exhaustive ordering nor to minimize any particular gift.

> *A healthy, fully functional church will desire and acquire all of God's gifts for His body.*

Of course, both in the human body and in the church some functions are more vital than others. The human body can survive without a foot but not without a beating heart. We should not choose between the two, however. A healthy body will have both, and both are necessary for the body to function as God intended. Likewise, the church could never have existed without the ministry of apostles, prophets, and teachers, yet it could limp along for a while without helps, administrations, and public messages in tongues. But that is no reason to despise the latter, or even to be content without them. A healthy, fully functional church will desire and acquire all of God's gifts for His body.

Verses 29-30 ask rhetorically if everyone holds certain ministerial offices or exercises certain supernatural gifts. The expected answer is no. (There is no example of the service gifts here, perhaps because this category is broad enough to encompass everyone.) Not everyone will hold one of the fivefold offices of Ephesians 4:11, and not everyone will exercise one of the supernatural gifts of I Corinthians 12:8-10. Nevertheless, everyone is important in the body of Christ.

We should note that verse 30 does not refer to tongues as the initial evidence of receiving the Holy Spirit. Instead, it means the gift of tongues in public worship for the benefit of the congregation, which should be accompanied by an interpretation. Indeed, the gift of interpretation is mentioned next. (For further discussion of this point, see chapter 12.)

"But earnestly desire the best gifts. And yet I show you a more excellent way" (verse 31).

The purpose of the preceding discussion is not to discourage the exercise of any gift. God intends for every body of believers to possess the full range of spiritual gifts. No single individual will necessarily exercise every gift, but the potential for each resides within him. Although not everyone will exercise spectacular gifts, all should earnestly seek the most valuable and needed gifts in their situation. If a local assembly completely lacks a certain gift, that would certainly be an important one for it to seek. (See discussion in chapter 4.)

And yet, as I Corinthians 13 explains, there is something even more important than desiring spiritual gifts, and that is possessing and manifesting divine love. Again, we should not choose one instead of the other, for God wants us to possess both the fruit of the Spirit—supremely love—and the gifts of the Spirit. But as a matter of priority, we must develop mature love before we can exercise spiritual gifts properly.

CHAPTER SIX

I CORINTHIANS 13:
LOVE IN THE EXERCISE
OF SPIRITUAL GIFTS

The theme of I Corinthians 13, one of the most quoted chapters of the Bible, is love. Significantly, it is placed in the middle of the discussion of spiritual gifts. God has thereby emphasized the priority of love over spiritual gifts and the necessity of love in exercising spiritual gifts. Let us analyze this passage with particular reference to the gifts.

SUPREMACY OF LOVE
(I CORINTHIANS 13:1-3)

"Though I speak with the tongues of men and of angels, but have not love, I have become as sounding brass or a clanging cymbal. And though I have the gift of prophecy, and understand all mysteries and all knowledge, and though I have all faith, so that I could

remove mountains, but have not love, I am nothing. And though I bestow all my goods to feed the poor, and though I give my body to be burned, but have not love, it profits me nothing."

The "more excellent way" of I Corinthians 12:31 is the way of love. I Corinthians 13 teaches the supremacy of love in the Christian life. No discussion of spiritual gifts is complete without considering love, for love is the necessary motive for every action.

The Greek word for love in this passage is *agape*, which in its highest sense means divine love, selfless love, sacrificial love, love without expectation of return. The King James Version translates it here as "charity," which was originally an excellent rendering. Over the centuries, however, charity came to refer primarily to aiding poor people, precisely because there was no thought of repayment.

To make its point, the passage cites several of the spiritual gifts of I Corinthians 12—tongues, prophecy, knowledge, faith—as well as good works. Indeed, it provides superlative examples: angelic as well as human tongues; comprehensive knowledge (not just a "word"), extending to all mysteries; complete faith, enough to move mountains; giving away all possessions; and the cruelest martyrdom. Even if one person manifests all these gifts and works to the ultimate degree, however, without love he is nothing and his deeds benefit him not at all. In our day, multitudes would flock to someone who exhibited such gifts and works, but Scripture warns us that, in themselves, none of these are the tests of spirituality and truth.

The only acceptable motive for operating spiritual gifts is love.

In short, the only acceptable motive for operating spiritual gifts is love. While we should earnestly desire spiritual gifts (I Corinthians 12:31), we must desire them for the right purpose: not to exalt ourselves but to bless others. Perhaps one reason why many Christians do not see more gifts in operation is because they desire them selfishly. (See James 4:3.)

When we exercise a spiritual gift, we must ask ourselves, Am I speaking or acting in love? Is my true motive love for God, His church, and the lost, or do I seek to enhance my ego?

Human motives can be a mixture of the selfish and the noble. Moreover, we humans have great ability to justify ourselves and deceive ourselves. Jeremiah 17:9 says, "The heart is deceitful above all things, and desperately wicked; who can know it?" None of us can trust his own heart, but we must periodically examine ourselves, ask the Lord to reveal secret impurities, and ask Him to purge us of improper motives and desires.

The psalmist displayed this attitude in prayer: "Who can understand his errors? Cleanse me from secret faults. Keep back Your servant also from presumptuous sins; let them not have dominion over me. Then I shall be blameless, and I shall be innocent of great transgression. Let the words of my mouth and the meditation of my heart be acceptable in Your sight, O LORD, my strength and my redeemer" (Psalm 19:12-14).

While we can and should have a strong desire for spiritual gifts, we must recognize that it is dangerous to pursue them without love. Because they are supernatural and often spectacular, we can easily seek them for personal attention or gain, ignoring what is best for others. We must continually remind ourselves, therefore, that without love all these gifts are meaningless.

CHARACTERISTICS OF LOVE
(I CORINTHIANS 13:4-7)

"Love suffers long and is kind; love does not envy; love does not parade itself, is not puffed up; does not behave rudely, does not seek its own, is not provoked, thinks no evil; does not rejoice in iniquity, but rejoices in the truth; bears all things, believes all things, hopes all things, endures all things."

These verses describe the essence of love, the kind of love that is necessary in the exercise of spiritual gifts. The following characteristics of love (using the words of the New International Version) will be displayed in the proper operation of spiritual gifts:

1. *Patient*
2. *Kind*

3. *Not envious*
4. *Not boastful*
5. *Not proud*
6. *Not rude*
7. *Not self-seeking*
8. *Not easily angered*
9. *Keeps no record of wrongs*
10. *Does not delight in evil*
11. *Rejoices in the truth*
12. *Always protects*
13. *Always trusts*
14. *Always hopes*
15. *Always perseveres*

Clearly, as verses 1-3 reveal, it is possible for someone to exercise spiritual gifts without love, which would be a misuse of them. The foregoing characteristics of love help us learn to use the gifts properly and help us identify improper uses. For instance, God never grants spiritual gifts for a hasty, harsh, rude, or hot-tempered rebuke. He does not give them to embarrass or humiliate others, to help someone get revenge, or to promote envy and strife. He does not give them to exalt the recipients or gratify their selfish desires. To the contrary, the proper use of spiritual gifts will always promote the truth of God's Word, protection of souls, trust in God, hope for the future, and perseverance in the faith.

If we are controlled by love, we will not misuse spiritual gifts. We will operate them as God wills, not for self-exaltation or self-gratification. We will not envy others whom God uses. We will not turn prophetic utterances into curses against people. We will not be swept into hero worship, false doctrine, or rebellion by spiritual manifestations, but our priorities will be to love God, to love truth, and to love souls.

PERMANENCE OF LOVE
(I CORINTHIANS 13:8-13)

"Love never fails. But whether there are prophecies, they will fail; whether there are tongues, they will cease; whether there is knowledge, it will vanish away. For we know in part and we prophesy in part. But when that which is perfect has come, then that which is in part will be done away. When I was a child, I spoke as a child, I understood as a child, I thought as a child; but when I became a man, I put away childish things. For now we see in a mirror, dimly, but then face to face. Now I know in part, but then I shall know just as I also am known. And now abide faith, hope, love, these three; but the greatest of these is love."

We should value love over spiritual gifts because only love is eternal. Only love is of the essence of the eternal kingdom of God. The permanence of love demonstrates its superiority over all other gifts and virtues.

When Christ catches away His church and establishes His eternal kingdom, we will no longer need the spiritual gifts, for we will attain full maturity and perfection in

Him. We will have perfect communion with God; thus we will not need tongues or prophecy. We will have full knowledge; thus we will not need partial knowledge ("the word of knowledge").

In this life, we walk by faith, not by sight (II Corinthians 5:7). We are saved in hope, for we cannot actually see our ultimate salvation yet (Romans 8:24-25). But one day, we will see all things clearly (I Corinthians 13:12). When the Lord returns for us, we will no longer need faith or hope, for our journey will be over and we will inherit all of God's promises. But love will still unite us with God and one another.

When the Lord returns for us, we will no longer need faith or hope, for our journey will be over.

Some theologians claim that the supernatural gifts, particularly tongues, have already ceased. If so, then we must also say on the basis of this passage that prophecy and partial knowledge have ceased, that we have perfect sight and knowledge, and by implication, that we no longer need faith or hope. Obviously, this view is erroneous.

The gifts will not cease until "that which is perfect," or "perfection" (NIV), comes. Some say "perfection" means the Bible, which became complete when the New Testament was finished. While the Bible is the complete

Word of God for us, neither the church nor the world has attained absolute perfection and will not do so until after the Lord comes back to earth. The New Testament age is not yet over, and the purposes for the gifts are still relevant.

> ## But love will still unite us with God and one another.

Moreover, in Greek "perfection" is *teleios*, which is neuter singular. But in Greek the complete Bible is spoken of as "the Scriptures." Twenty times the New Testament uses *graphai*, which is feminine plural, and once it uses *grammata*, which is neuter plural. Grammatically, neither word agrees with *teleios*, so it could not be a pronoun that substitutes for "the Scriptures."

I Corinthians 1:7 has already established that the gifts will endure until the Second Coming. "Perfection" must refer to this event or to the kingdom that Christ will establish at His coming.

Someone has said that faith rests on the past, hope looks to the future, but love works in the present. Love is the most important of the three because it operates in the eternal now.

CHAPTER SEVEN

WISDOM, KNOWLEDGE, AND DISCERNING OF SPIRITS

N ow let us turn to a discussion of each of the gifts of I Corinthians 12. The first three we will consider are the word of wisdom, the word of knowledge, and the discerning of spirits. For the sake of study we will identify them as *the gifts of revelation*, because they involve a direct impartation of insight or understanding from the mind of God to us.

WORD OF WISDOM

The first gift listed in I Corinthians 12 is "the word of wisdom." The Greek word for "wisdom" here is the standard one, *sophia*. "Wisdom" means "understanding of what is true, right, or lasting; insight; . . . common sense; good judgment." Knowledge is an understanding of facts, but wisdom is an understanding of how to use facts to make good decisions. Wisdom involves insight, judgment, guidance.

God does not impart all His wisdom but a "word," or a portion, of wisdom. The Greek for "word" here is *logos*, which typically refers to thought or utterance. The gift of "the word of wisdom" does not bestow infallibility or divine guidance in all matters, but it relates to a specific decision or need.

> *The word of wisdom is the supernatural gift of a portion of divine insight, judgment, or guidance for a particular need.*

Based on the words of I Corinthians 12:8 as well as the entire context of I Corinthians 12-14, we can define the word of wisdom as *the supernatural gift of a portion of divine insight, judgment, or guidance for a particular need.*

God has worked miraculously throughout human history, and therefore we can find parallels to the gifts of the Spirit in the Old Testament and in the Gospels. Since the gifts of I Corinthians 12 are given to New Testament believers, who are baptized with the Holy Spirit, we can expect to find specific instances of them in the Book of Acts and the Epistles.

We find an example of the word of wisdom in the story of the apostle Paul's voyage to Rome as a prisoner. Although Paul was not a professional sailor, the Lord revealed to him that it was unwise to sail further, and he communicated this message to the Roman centurion in charge of him, the helmsman, and the owner of the ship. "Now when much time had been spent, and sailing was now dangerous because the Fast was already over, Paul advised them, saying, 'Men, I perceive that this voyage will end with disaster and much loss, not only of the cargo and ship, but also our lives'" (Acts 27:9-10).

The professionals, however, concluded that it was safe to sail, and the south wind began to blow softly, seemingly confirming their opinion. They ignored Paul's words and set sail. Soon they encountered a violent tempest in which they lost both the cargo and the ship. They would have lost their lives also except for the intervention of God and the further advice of Paul.

In this account, human understanding, experience, and observation said it was safe to sail, and Paul had no expertise or human reason to think otherwise. Yet by divine wisdom, Paul knew it was dangerous to go. God gave him supernatural guidance apart from human judgment. Even though the centurion ignored Paul's advice initially, the word of wisdom gave him such credibility in light of later events that in the end everyone did heed his instructions for the preservation of their lives.

Another instance of the word of wisdom is when the Holy Spirit guided Paul and his coworkers in their missionary endeavors. The Spirit forbade them to go to Asia or Bithynia at that time; then God gave Paul a vision of someone from Macedonia asking for help. The missionary party concluded that God wanted them to go to

Macedonia. (See Acts 16:6-10.)

In 1976, while my father was a missionary in South Korea, some opponents of the church sought to have him expelled from the country, the church organization dissolved, and the assets awarded to them. They falsely accused him to the government of plotting to assassinate the president. At that time the country was strictly controlled by a military dictatorship and lived under constant threat of attack by communist North Korea. Acts of espionage were common, and once a team of North Korean commandos almost reached the president's house before being discovered and killed in downtown gun battles. In 1974 a communist agent killed the president's wife in a failed attempt to assassinate him. There was also considerable unrest due to domestic political opposition. In that environment, the South Korean Central Intelligence Agency took this allegation very seriously. Indeed the president was later assassinated.

My father was scheduled to preach soon at the first world conference of the United Pentecostal Church International, to be held in Jerusalem. In prayer, however, he felt impressed by the Holy Spirit not to go, so he canceled his travel plans.

Afterwards, the Korean CIA conducted an extensive investigation, which included the brutal interrogation of some students of the Bible college where my father was president. Eventually the minister of justice called my father into his office and notified him of the outcome. The government knew of my father's planned trip, he said, and initially decided that the easiest solution to the problem was to deny him reentry to Korea after the trip. They did not want to create an international incident by expelling him, but they did not want him to remain in the country as a potential threat. Since he did not take the trip, they were forced to investigate, and their investigation revealed that his accusers were liars.

God granted him divine guidance, and as a result the crisis was resolved.

My father had no human way of knowing these plans and no human reason to cancel his trip. Yet God granted him divine guidance, and as a result the crisis was resolved. The plan of the conspirators was thwarted.

In my own life, I have felt specific direction from God on a number of occasions. In 1981, I obtained ministerial license; graduated from the University of Texas School of Law in Austin, Texas; married; and moved to Jackson, Mississippi, to begin teaching at Jackson College of Ministries. As my wife and I left Austin, I told her I felt impressed that someday we would come back to Austin to work for the Lord. Over the years, we carried a burden for the city, and I was approached on four occasions about ministerial positions there: to start a daughter work, to be assistant pastor, and to be pastor of two different churches. In 1986 we seriously contemplated starting a new church there, consulting with family, friends, spiritual leaders, the sectional presbyter, and the district superintendent. All human signs were encouraging, yet we did not feel positive direction from the Lord, so we did not go.

In 1991, our burden intensified. Once again, we began praying, seeking counsel, and gathering necessary information. As my wife and I prayed together on December 31, the Spirit of God came upon us. I asked God to fulfill Romans 8:26 in our lives: "For we do not know what we should pray for as we ought, but the Spirit Himself makes intercession for us with groanings which cannot be uttered." Immediately, I felt as if a heavy weight pressed down upon my chest, almost as if I were drowning, and I began to sob and to speak forcefully in tongues. We knew God had answered our prayer and would soon give us direction. Two days later, on January 2, 1992, in prayer my wife and I both felt a strong sense of victory and a confirmation that we were to make plans immediately to begin a new church in Austin. After approval by the district board, we went.

God gave us supernatural direction at the right time.

In retrospect, the timing could not have been better. Unknown to us, about the same time we moved to Austin several families also moved there who were to become building blocks of our new church, including a family who had received the Holy Spirit in the charismatic movement and one who was holding prayer meetings in their home.

In the late 1980s, Austin suffered a severe economic decline, but in the early 1990s it began an unprecedented boom. We were able to buy a home and land for a church just before real estate prices skyrocketed. In two years, our land was worth almost double the purchase price. Humanly speaking, we could not have anticipated, planned, or orchestrated these and many other events to bring our church to its present level of growth and revival, but God gave us supernatural direction at the right time.

The word of knowledge is the supernatural gift of a portion of divine information for a particular need.

WORD OF KNOWLEDGE

The second gift in I Corinthians 12 is "the word of knowledge." The Greek word for "knowledge" here is the standard one, *gnosis*. "Knowledge" means "familiarity, awareness, or understanding gained through experience or study; . . . the sum or range of what has been perceived, discovered, or learned." This gift involves a revelation of divine information to someone who does not know it by natural means. While another person may know it, the recipient obtains it from the Spirit.

Like the word of wisdom, the "word" of knowledge is not all the knowledge of God, but a portion of God's knowledge. From the text and context of I Corinthians 12-14, we can define the word of knowledge as *the supernatural gift of a portion of divine information for a particular need.*

Acts 5:1-10 provides an example of this gift: "But a certain man named Ananias, with Sapphira his wife, sold a possession. And he kept back part of the proceeds, his wife also being aware of it, and brought a certain part and laid it at the apostles' feet. But Peter said, 'Ananias, why has Satan filled your heart to lie to the Holy Spirit and keep back part of the price of the land for yourself? While it remained, was it not your own? And after it was sold, was it not in your own control? Why have you conceived this thing in your heart? You have not lied to men but to God.' Then Ananias, hearing these words, fell down and breathed his last. . . . Now it was about three hours later when his wife came in, not knowing what had happened. And Peter answered her, 'Tell me whether you sold the land for so much?' And she said, 'Yes, for so much.' Then Peter said to her, 'How is it that you have agreed together to test the Spirit of the Lord? Look, the feet of those who have buried your husband are at the door, and they will carry you out.' Then immediately she fell down at his feet and breathed her last."

Here, God miraculously revealed to the apostle Peter secret information known only to Ananias and Sapphira. They pretended to give the total price of their land to the church when actually they gave only a part. While it was their right to keep some or all of the money, they sinned by lying to the church, and God disclosed the truth to

Peter. After Ananias died, God revealed to Peter that Sapphira would receive the same judgment.

God miraculously revealed to the apostle Peter secret information.

In Korea, my mother and two other ministers were walking to a remote coastal village to pray for a pastor who was seriously ill. (My father had to attend an important meeting with the Ministry of Cultural Affairs and Education, which had jurisdiction over missionary work.) The ministers took a shortcut through the rice paddies, a path unknown to my mother. Soon snow began to fall heavily until visibility was almost zero. The travelers began falling into the irrigation ditches along the sides of the path. What should have been a forty-five-minute walk turned into two hours with no end in sight. The party was completely lost.

My mother began to pray earnestly, and the Lord impressed her to go in the opposite direction. Her companions strongly objected, saying that path would lead to the Yellow Sea, which would be dangerous. My mother insisted that God had spoken to her and she would go that direction. Reluctantly, the others followed. After another hour of walking they spotted the lights of the village they sought. Their hands were so numb that they could not knock on the door, but they had arrived safely by a word of knowledge.

While in Korea, my parents conducted English services for American soldiers in addition to their full-time missionary work among the Koreans. One day a soldier and the teenage son of a sergeant major came to their house for prayer. As they entered the door, God revealed to my father that the soldier was a homosexual. In private counsel with my parents, the man admitted his homosexuality, and my father took steps to ensure that he would not be alone with any of the young men.

At the close of an evangelistic service one Sunday night in Hammond, Louisiana, my mother was strongly impressed of God that someone needed to make a definite decision that night. She told the congregation, "There is someone here who should not leave this building without talking to God. I feel a heavy burden about this." A few weeks later, a construction worker who was in the service was injured on the job and died.

"You prayed exactly according to my needs."

On another occasion in Gonzales, Louisiana, my mother was counseling a woman who had received the Holy Spirit but who continued to live a sinful life. The Spirit of God came upon my mother and revealed that something serious was going to happen to the woman if she did not repent. Within one week she was in the hospital with a paralyzed arm and leg. After she repented in the hospital room and fully dedicated her life to God, God healed her.

A number of times I have felt impressed to make specific requests while praying with people. Later some have told me, "You prayed exactly according to my needs," even though I had no human knowledge of them or their situations. In 1994, I spoke at a retreat for ministers and wives in Pennsylvania. The Lord moved powerfully in the last session, and I began praying for various people. Afterwards a senior pastor told me, "I noticed that you walked straight to a young minister from our church, passing everyone else, and laid your hands on him. He faces a crisis and must make an important decision. The words you prayed matched his situation exactly."

In 1997, a first-time visitor with an urgent need came to our church in Austin. The church she usually attended taught the baptism of the Holy Spirit, but most of the members had not received this experience. The previous Sunday the pastor and entire congregation had prayed with this woman, but she had not felt the power of God. When she visited our church, I was led to pray with her personally. Later she told the person who had invited her, "He prayed exactly according to my needs, and God touched me. I know God directed his prayers."

While I was preaching in Austin one Sunday morning, in the middle of my message I felt to say, "If there is someone here today who does not know whether God exists or not, God will reveal Himself to you if you will ask Him to do so." Unknown to me, a first-time visitor had walked in late, just before I made this statement. After service, she told me, "I was raised in a traditional denomination, and I know how to use all the correct religious language. No one else, not even my own family, has any idea of what I am going to tell you, but I do not know if God exists or not. Do you think He will truly reveal Himself to me?" I answered that He had already begun to do so, for He had spoken to her through my message. Later she had a personal encounter with God, was baptized in the name of Jesus, and was filled with the Holy Spirit.

DISCERNING OF SPIRITS

I Corinthians 12:10 lists the gift of "discerning of spirits." Like the other two gifts we have discussed, it involves a disclosure from God but not a revelation of all the mind of God. It is not a general gift of discernment but specifically a discerning of spirits.

The word "discernment" means "keenness of insight and judgment." It refers to the ability to make a proper distinction or determination, such as to know truth from error. The discerning of spirits, then, involves keen insight and judgment with regard to spirits.

There are three possible sources of a spiritual activity: God and His angels, the devil and his demons, or the human spirit. Through discerning of spirits, we are able to understand which one has motivated a certain action. This gift can also provide information about the type of spirit that underlies certain actions, such as a spirit of lust, envy, or greed. This knowledge can be invaluable in dealing with or responding to certain situations. In summary, discerning of spirits is *the supernatural gift of perceiving the spiritual motivations for an action, or what type of spirit is at work.*

Discerning of spirits is the supernatural gift of perceiving the spiritual motivations for an action, or what type of spirit is at work.

We find a notable example of this gift in Paul's ministry at Philippi. "Now it happened, as we went to prayer, that a certain slave girl possessed with a spirit of divination met us, who brought her masters much profit by fortune-telling. This girl followed Paul and us, and cried out, saying, 'These men are the servants of the Most High God, who proclaim to us the way of salvation.' And this she did for many days. But Paul, greatly annoyed, turned and said to the spirit, 'I command you in the name of Jesus Christ to come out of her.' And he came out that very hour" (Acts 16:16-18).

Paul discerned that this girl was demon possessed. Had he not perceived the truth about her, he might have accepted her accolades. But if he had, he would have associated the gospel message with demonic activity and would have been discredited in the eyes of the people.

On the first missionary journey of Barnabas and Paul, they encountered a false prophet named Elymas in

Paphos on the island of Cyprus. When they witnessed to the Roman proconsul, Elymas tried to turn the man away from the truth. But "Paul, filled with the Holy Spirit, looked intently at him and said, 'O full of all deceit and all fraud, you son of the devil, you enemy of all right-eousness, will you not cease perverting the straight ways of the Lord? And now, indeed, the hand of the Lord is upon you, and you shall be blind, not seeing the sun for a time.' And immediately a dark mist fell on him, and he went around seeking someone to lead him by the hand" (Acts 13:9-11). Through discerning of spirits Paul per-ceived the evil intent and work of this false prophet, and through the word of knowledge he knew the judgment of God that would soon befall him. As a result of these gifts of the Spirit, the proconsul became a believer.

Human sin is primarily the result of the sinful human nature, human lusts, and human choices.

It is important to know when an evil spirit is at work, but it is an error to attribute every sin or wrong action to the direct work of an evil spirit. While the devil tempts us to sin and takes full advantage of wrong deci-sions and actions, human sin is primarily the result of the sinful human nature, human lusts, and human choic-es. (See Romans 3:9-12; James 1:14-15.) Many prob-lems or mistakes do not come directly from the devil but from the human spirit.

For instance, let us suppose a person attempts to speak to the church in tongues, interpretation, or prophecy, but the leader of the service realizes the words are not of God. If they are prompted by an evil spirit, he needs to take firm control of the service and rebuke the evil spirit. On the other hand, it may be that the words come from the human zeal of a sincere but misguided Christian. In such a case, it would be better to conduct a smooth transition to worship or prayer and to instruct the untrained Christian at a later time. If the leader acts too harshly, he may unnecessarily wound the sincere person or others in the service. Discerning of spirits is valuable in such cases.

In Jackson, Mississippi, a man came to pray at the altar and soon began bucking, kicking, and writhing as if demon possessed. A number of men gathered to pray with him, restrain him, and rebuke the devil. Nothing seemed to help. Finally, the pastor walked over to him and whispered in his ear. Immediately the man ceased his disruptive behavior and walked out of the church. The pastor did not issue a powerful rebuke in Jesus' name but simply told him, "If you do not stop acting like this, I'm going to call the police." He perceived that the man was trying to create a scene and get attention. It was a carnal, not a demonic, display, and it needed to be handled accordingly.

In a church in Houston, Texas, a woman suddenly stood up and began speaking in tongues in the middle of a service I attended. The pastor discerned that she was motivated by an evil spirit. He immediately said, "Sit down. That is not of God." Then he continued with the service as if nothing had happened. The congregation recognized the appropriateness of his action and the service progressed positively. If the pastor had allowed the speaking to continue, or if he had allowed the devil to distract him by a prolonged confrontation with the woman, the service would have suffered and God's purpose would not have been accomplished.

When my parent were home missionaries in Hammond, Louisiana, at the close of a service my mother was praying with sinners at the altar while my father was greeting visitors. A woman began speaking in tongues loudly and approached the altar. Simultaneously, both my parents discerned that she was speaking by an evil spirit. Without any other signal, they both began walking toward her to stop her from further disruption. They later discovered that she was living a very sinful life and bringing reproach upon the true gift of the Holy Spirit by her deceptive manifestations. A similar incident occurred in a revival service in Korea.

As a senior in high school in Korea, I was hiking across a mountain with some of my classmates. As we passed a Buddhist temple on the mountain, we encountered a man and an elderly woman who had just emerged from worshiping there. The man was beating the woman, but as we approached he stopped and the woman escaped. Since some girls in my class were still several minutes behind me, I decided to wait for them in case the man attempted to harass them. As I watched the man from some distance away, I felt an evil spirit in him, and I thought he might attack me. I looked directly at him and softly began saying in English, "I rebuke you in the name of Jesus." Although he probably could not hear me and probably could not speak English, suddenly the man spoke to me in English, "I hate your eyes! I hate your eyes!" He kept his distance, however, and all my classmates passed by safely. I believe the Spirit of God in me restrained him, and he felt that opposition.

A woman in our church in Austin suffered from chronic depression, which undermined her faith in God. Through a long process we were able to convince her that God loved her and that she could be filled with the Holy Spirit, and after a year she did receive the Spirit. Later, however, she reverted to her depressed state, doubted that she had ever received the Holy Spirit, and even doubted that she had ever felt God's presence although on several occasions she had experienced dramatic physical manifestations of trembling and falling under the power of God. She stopped attending church, but I convinced her to come to the last of a series of special services. In church, the evangelist called upon her, stated that she was troubled by a spirit of depression, and prayed for her deliverance. She claimed victory that night and in a totally uncharacteristic way began to run up and down the aisles praising God ecstatically. Since that time she has been faithful in attendance, joyful in worship, and determined to keep her victory.

At a jail service, two workers from our church in Austin prayed for a prisoner who began to seek God.

Independently, both men discerned that he struggled with a spirit of homosexuality. After a while, he told one of them he needed deliverance but did not say what his problem was. One of the workers then asked if he needed deliverance from homosexuality, and he said yes. When they prayed, a visible transformation came over his countenance, and he began speaking in tongues as the Spirit gave utterance. He later testified that God had set him free from homosexual desires.

Summary

Like all the supernatural gifts, the gifts of revelation are potentially available to every Spirit-filled believer. In times of decision, urgent need, or crisis, each of us should call on the Lord to grant us supernatural wisdom, knowledge, or discerning of spirits as the occasion requires.

The gifts of revelation are potentially available to every Spirit-filled believer.

By their very nature, we would expect these gifts to be most valuable to those in spiritual leadership. Often God will give a pastor supernatural guidance for a difficult decision, supernatural knowledge concerning a hidden problem in the church, or discernment concerning a spirit that is opposing his ministry.

The three gifts we have discussed are closely related, and there can be some overlapping of them. One person may interpret a certain instance as the manifestation of one of the gifts while another person may consider it to be a different gift. Regardless of our precise classification, we can all recognize it as the work of the Holy Spirit.

As we discussed in chapter 2, the gifts of revelation are supernatural, but they have counterparts in everyday natural and spiritual life. Everyone, even sinners, can have earthly wisdom, knowledge, and discernment. Moreover, every Christian can and should attain spiritual wisdom, knowledge, and discernment. In addition to these two levels, however, there are the supernatural gifts of the word of wisdom, the word of knowledge, and discerning of spirits that operate at special times of need. To function as God intends and to thwart the stratagems of Satan, the church needs these gifts at work today.

CHAPTER EIGHT

FAITH AND MIRACLES

The next three gifts we will discuss are *the gifts of power*—faith, gifts of healings, and the working of miracles (I Corinthians 12:9-10). We use this description because these gifts involve visible works that come by the power of God.

These gifts often work closely together. For instance the gift of faith may lead to the working of a miracle.

FAITH

Faith means confidence, trust, acceptance without tangible proof, reliance, commitment. Every child of God possesses saving faith and lives daily by faith (Romans 1:16-17). In addition, every Christian should manifest faith, or faithfulness, as the fruit of the Spirit (Galatians 5:22). But I Corinthians 12 describes a supernatural gift of faith that transcends the faith required for salvation and Christian living. While everyone can and should exercise faith in God on a continual basis, the gift of faith is an extraordinary measure of faith for an individual in a special situation.

> *The gift of faith is the supernatural ability to trust God, or to inspire trust in God, for a particular need or circumstance.*

The gift of faith, then, is *the supernatural ability to trust God, or to inspire trust in God, for a particular need or circumstance.* It often comes in response to a trial or a crisis that would overwhelm a person except that God grants special faith to overcome in spite of the circumstances. It may be a situation in which there is apparently no escape, but God gives faith to move a mountain out of the way.

When Paul was shipwrecked in Acts 27, the sailors lost all hope of life. But an angel appeared to Paul and assured him that God would deliver him and his fellow travelers. In Acts 27:25 Paul spoke confidently to them: "Take heart, men, for I believe God that it will be just as it was told me." Although there was no human reason to have hope, God gave Paul the ability to believe for protection and deliverance in the impossible situation, not only for himself but for the unbelievers on board also.

In such a situation, a child of God, who is filled with

the Holy Spirit, could nevertheless think that disaster will strike. A person could have total confidence in God and yet conclude that the end of his life had come. Indeed, this conclusion would be the only logical one under the circumstances. In other words, faith for salvation and Christian living does not automatically result in faith for a miraculous deliverance.

The gift of faith may operate even when no miraculous deliverance is forthcoming. Stephen was "full of faith and the Holy Spirit" (Acts 6:5), and he exhibited an incredible faith when he was stoned to death, faith beyond the ordinary ability of humans. Instead of displaying fear, anger, bitterness, or pain, he faced martyrdom courageously and with a Christ-like spirit of forgiveness, enabled by the Holy Spirit. "He, being full of the Holy Spirit, gazed into heaven and saw the glory of God, and Jesus standing at the right hand of God. . . . Then he knelt down and cried out with a loud voice, 'Lord, do not charge them with this sin.' And when he had said this, he fell asleep" (Acts 7:55, 60).

In 1978 a cousin of mine who was a preacher was killed at age twenty-four in a tragic accident in Alabama. A preacher friend of his shot him by mistake while they were hunting together. My uncle, the father of the slain man, had lost his wife to cancer five years earlier; she was in her forties. The friend who had accidentally killed my cousin came to the funeral home where the body lay but was understandably reluctant to see the family.

When my uncle heard he was there, he insisted on meeting him. Although grieving deeply himself, he ministered to the young man, telling him, in essence, "Do not torture yourself with guilt. Satan would like to use this event to destroy your ministry, but you must go forward, do the work God has called you to do, and help fulfill the unfinished work of my son. God could have miraculously blocked this accident, but He did not, and we must accept what has happened. I forgive you for your mistake. Now we both must place everything in God's hands." Then they prayed together, weeping and speaking in tongues. Surely it was the gift of faith that enabled my uncle to act in such a Christ-like manner under the bleakest of circumstances.

In 1980, the church in Korea faced an urgent need for Bible college facilities. My parents obtained special permission from the Foreign Missions Board to travel in America to raise the necessary funds even though their regularly scheduled furlough had not yet come. After traveling for three months they were still far short of what they needed. One night they attended the annual camp meeting in Louisiana and sat toward the back of the tabernacle. In the middle of his message, the evening speaker felt impressed to stop and make an appeal for their need. He took a check from his pocket, which represented the price of a truck he had sold that day, and gave it toward the Bible college project.

A spirit of sacrifice swept the congregation, and people streamed to the front with sacrificial gifts, including cash, tape recorders, watches, rings, and coats. In about ten minutes, the crowd gave fifty-five thousand dollars, enough to meet the need. This offering transcended human generosity; it was divinely orchestrated. A spirit of extraordinary faith began in the speaker and overwhelmed the congregation as they reached beyond themselves and allowed God to work through them to accomplish His purpose.

A spirit of extraordinary faith began in the speaker and overwhelmed the congregation.

When I was a teacher and administrator at Jackson College of Ministries, we employed an independent Baptist minister who had recently been baptized in the name of Jesus Christ and filled with the Holy Spirit. An African-American, he had many contacts in the black religious community and a strong burden to see his friends and associates receive the same message and experience that had transformed his life. Together, in 1985, we designed a plan to reach them. Since he knew many ministers who wanted theological training but did not have an opportunity to obtain it, we decided to offer an evening class called "The Theology of Acts." About twenty preachers and deacons enrolled. In addition to the two of us who organized the class, several others had already been baptized with the Holy Spirit, but most had not.

I began at Acts 1 and taught on repentance, water baptism in Jesus' name, the baptism of the Holy Spirit, speaking in tongues, and so on. At the conclusion of the fourth lesson, I felt the time was ripe for God to move in a special way. I acknowledged my students' previous experience with God but urged them to press on to receive everything God had for them. I explained that the only way to do so was not by trusting in past accomplishments but by approaching God in humility, repentance, and surrender. I asked everyone who wanted the fullness of the Spirit and who wanted an apostolic ministry to stand and step forward. Then I told them to confess all sin to God and yield their lives completely. After they had done so, they were to begin praising God and thanking Him for His promise. Their praise would be the sign that they were ready to receive the Holy Spirit, and I would lay hands on them according to the examples in the Book of Acts. At that point, they were to believe God for the baptism of the Holy Spirit.

A transcendent faith permeated the classroom.

As we followed this simple plan, faith began to rise and the power of God fell. No one told the students that they had to tarry for hours, days, weeks, or months, or that they had to seek the Lord many times before the Holy Spirit would come. They only knew what I had shown them in the Bible. We all began to pray, and in about fifteen minutes five preachers and deacons received the Holy Spirit with the initial sign of speaking in tongues. A transcendent faith permeated the classroom, working through the Spirit-filled members and inspiring others to receive their own personal Pentecost.

WORKING OF MIRACLES

A miracle is "an event that appears inexplicable by the laws of nature and so is held to be supernatural in origin or an act of God." It is an extraordinary, unusual occurrence that suspends or transcends the laws of nature as we know them. It involves the direct intervention of God. Of course, to God all things are possible, and what is a miracle to us is standard procedure for Him. God is the Creator, and as such He can work in ways that are impossible for us.

The working of miracles is the supernatural intervention of God that transcends the laws of nature in a situation and operates through or with a human vessel.

In a general sense, all answers to prayer, all spiritual gifts, and all divine healings are miraculous. (See, for example, Acts 19:11-12.) Yet I Corinthians 12 lists "the working of miracles" as a specific gift different from the others, including healings. The word "working" (Greek, *energema*) indicates a specific operation of God, and since "the working of miracles" is a gift "to" someone, it indicates an operation through, with, or by means of, a member of Christ's body. God can do miracles in the lives of sinners, but the gift of the working of miracles denotes the action of God through His church. In short, the working of miracles is *the supernatural intervention of God that transcends the laws of nature in a situation and operates through or with a human vessel.*

The New Testament church received the working of miracles on numerous occasions. The Spirit transported Philip from the desert of Gaza to Azotus (Acts 8:39-40). An angel miraculously delivered Peter from prison as the church prayed for him (Acts 12:5-11). Demons were expelled out of possessed people (Acts 8:6-7; 19:11-12). A young man named Eutychus went to sleep during a long sermon of Paul's, fell from a third-story seat, broke his neck, and died, but after Paul ministered personally to him, he rose up from the dead (Acts 20:9-12). More than the healing of a sickness or handicap, this event was a miracle of resurrection and restoration to natural life. Similarly, God raised Tabitha (Dorcas) from the dead through the prayers of Peter (Acts 9:36-42). Paul was miraculously protected from harm when a poisonous snake bit him (Acts 28:3-6).

Some miracles are evident only to those who believe, whereas unbelievers will offer a natural explanation or give credit to luck or coincidence. Other miracles, however, defy all rational explanation.

By definition, miracles are extraordinary and exceptional. As with all the spiritual gifts, we should expect the working of miracles, but we must not think we can operate our entire lives by this gift. For instance, despite Philip's miracle, the apostles did not rely on the Spirit as their normal means of transportation. Most first-century Christians who were arrested were not miraculously delivered from prison, and most who died were not raised up.

Some people today expect God to supply all their needs in a miraculous fashion, but He has a more mundane plan for everyday life, which includes hard work, good stewardship, and giving of tithes and offerings. The general principle is, "If anyone will not work, neither shall he eat" (II Thessalonians 3:10). Some are envious of the houses and cars of others but fail to recognize that, while God is the one who has blessed the owners, in many cases these possessions resulted from years of hard work, discipline, frugality, saving, and planning.

We should trust God to supply our needs, expecting answers to prayer and the working of miracles, but we should not neglect our daily responsibility to act prudently in accordance with the laws of nature, society, and economics. We do not demonstrate faith by inaction but by works—by doing everything we can do and everything we know to do.

The miracles in the early church not only met genuine needs, but they were particularly effective in spreading the gospel. (See Acts 9:42.) God still grants miracles today as an effective means of furthering the truth and strengthening the church.

When I began working at Jackson College of Ministries in 1981, the school had just undergone a traumatic change of administration and was in spiritual and financial crisis. Over the next four years God helped us rebuild from a low enrollment of 163 to a record of 292. Humanly speaking, however, in the first few semesters the survival of the school was in doubt. Indeed, at one point, the president secretly entered into negotiations to sell the facility to another group. Throughout this time, many people prayed earnestly for God to meet the needs.

Just before the president was to meet with the potential buyers, a Methodist man from a nearby neighborhood walked into my office. He wanted to pay tithes on a large income from a major construction project. He had moved into a new house elsewhere but was unable to sell his old house, so he came up with the idea of donating it as a means of paying his tithes. His church did not need a parsonage, but as he was driving down the road he spotted our college and decided that we might have such a need. After a few minutes of preliminary talk, he offered to give his house to our school.

I contacted our vice president to arrange to meet with the owner and view the house. On the way, the owner casually asked our church affiliation. The vice president told him that we were Pentecostal but, in an attempt to build rapport, explained that we were much like the old-time Methodists. The man replied that he was a modern Methodist but did not withdraw his offer. At the official transfer of the property, his wife remarked, as she signed the documents with him, that she did not know what made him decide to give the house to us.

From our perspective, his gift was a miracle from God in response to much prayer. After selling the house and paying off the remaining indebtedness, the college made a profit of about sixty thousand dollars. Not only did this donation meet the immediate financial need, but it provided decisive encouragement and confirmation at a crucial time.

His gift was a miracle from God.

In 1988, our missionary to Eastern Europe asked me to accompany him to Bulgaria, then a strict communist country, to conduct the first meetings there to be sponsored by the United Pentecostal Church. He had recently made contact with a sizable group of underground believers who had received the Holy Spirit and who were interested in our message. We traveled by car from Austria through Yugoslavia and carried a manuscript of my book *The Oneness of God* translated into Bulgarian. We put it on the back dash under a package, hoping the border guards would consider us as tourists and not search us carefully. We knew a thorough search would surely uncover the manuscript, and the more carefully it was hidden the more incriminating it would look when found. If they determined that we had deliberately tried to smuggle contraband, the consequences for us could be severe.

When we arrived at the border, the captain of the

guard singled out our car for a special search. We had to drive into a garage where a guard searched the car from front to back, under the hood, and under the chassis. He questioned me closely concerning a *National Geographic* magazine that I carried for leisure reading. He was so concerned over this harmless piece of literature that I dreaded his reaction when he discovered the openly religious document we had. I prayed silently and smiled outwardly. As the guard continued his search, he uncovered the manuscript, and his hand brushed across it. It lay in full view, with the Bulgarian title clearly readable, yet he never saw it. After over one hour of searching, the guard finally waved us on. We knew God had protected us by a miracle.

We knew God had protected us by a miracle.

My wife and I and our two boys traveled in our minivan from Austin to St. Louis after Christmas in December 1990. In Oklahoma we encountered ice on the interstate highway, and I slowed down. Unfortunately, a truck behind us continued at a high speed, passed us, and suddenly swerved in front of us to avoid colliding with another truck and trailer that had just begun fishtailing across the road. I delayed braking until the last moment.

As soon as I braked, I lost control of my van and knew a wreck was imminent. My wife cried out, "Jesus!"

At that moment, the truck ahead of us jackknifed, slid off the road, and stopped without causing a wreck or injuring anyone. I regained control of our van, and we continued on, praising God for His protection. We had literally come within inches of a major collision.

In the meantime, my mother-in-law in Austin had heard about the weather conditions where we were driving and was greatly troubled. She prayed under a heavy burden until God gave her a vision of our van nestled under the care of an angel. Her vision itself was a miracle, and it confirmed to us that God had performed a miracle of protection in our moment of need.

In October 1995, at a prayer meeting in our church in Austin, God spoke to us in tongues and interpretation at a critical time and promised that we would soon see a miracle. Five days later, in a missions service, my wife's grandfather slumped over in his seat and became unconscious. He stopped breathing, lost all color, and had no pulse. His body was limp, his jaw slack, his eyes rolled back, and his skin clammy. We gathered around him and began to call on the name of Jesus.

At first, there was no response, but as we continued praying he coughed and began to breathe again. By the time the emergency medical personnel arrived, he was conscious and joking, his color had returned, and all vital signs were normal.

After extensive testing at the hospital, the doctors found no indications of a stroke, heart attack, or other life-threatening event, but they did discover ninety-nine percent blockage in his carotid artery and performed immediate surgery. While in the hospital, he suffered a slight stroke, from which he mostly recovered.

Since they could never find any damage, the doctors concluded that at church he must have merely fainted. We who were there, however, were convinced that he reached the point of death itself, probably due to a massive stroke, but the Lord miraculously intervened, arrested and reversed the stroke, and raised him up from the dead.

CHAPTER NINE

HEALING

In addition to faith and the working of miracles, the gifts of power include "the gifts of healing" (KJV) or "gifts of healings" (NKJV) (I Corinthians 12:9). "To heal" means "to restore to health or soundness; cure; . . . to set right; repair; . . . to restore (a person) to . . . wholeness."

In the broadest sense, healing can refer to physical, mental, and spiritual restoration. At the conversion experience, all Christians receive spiritual healing, including forgiveness of sins, reconciliation with God, and new spiritual life. As they grow in grace, they begin to develop positive emotional and spiritual attributes such as love, peace, joy, and self-control, which the Bible calls the fruit of the Spirit (Galatians 5:22-23).

I Corinthians 12, however, speaks of specific instances of healing that are given to certain individuals but not to everyone. The reference is to healing of physical and mental conditions beyond the spiritual and emotional restoration that all Christians can and should receive as part of their new life in Christ. The examples of healing in the Gospels and Acts correspond to this meaning.

The gifts of healing are various forms of supernatural cure or restoration from illnesses, diseases, injuries, and other impairments.

This gift is the only one listed in the plural form; actually there are many gifts of healing. The plural indicates that there are various kinds of healing—both different conditions that are healed and different ways in which healing takes place. With these points in mind, we can define the gifts of healing as *various forms of supernatural cure or restoration from illnesses, diseases, injuries, and other impairments.*

There are numerous accounts of healing in the New Testament church, including that of a lame man at the Temple; multitudes in Jerusalem; many paralyzed and lame people in Samaria; Saul of Tarsus, who was healed of blindness; and a bedridden man named Aeneas in Lydda (Acts 3:1-8; 5:14-16; 8:7; 9:17-18, 32-34).

Many miraculous healings have occurred in my parents' life and ministry. In 1963, as my family was preparing to go to Korea, we were involved in a serious automobile accident that caused many injuries. Both my father's arms were broken, and the nerve in his right arm was severed. For months he had no control of his right hand, and his doctor told him he would never be able to use it again. Much to the doctor's amazement, however, one night in church God completely healed my father's hand, immediately restoring it to full use.

In Mokpo, Korea, a man was instantly healed of a paralyzed arm and shoulder as my father prayed with him. In Seoul, Korea, a woman was delivered from voices that constantly spoke violent words and curses in her mind, and a twelve-year-old girl was healed of a severe hearing impairment. I was in the service on each of these occasions and saw the healed person. A lame woman came in a wheelchair to a crusade in downtown Seoul and was healed; I watched as she walked joyfully across the stage of the rented auditorium. Other notable, instantaneous healings in Korea were those of a man with a deaf ear, a girl with tuberculosis who had lost the use of one lung and most of the other, and a woman in the last stages of breast cancer.

In 1984, I preached in Poplarville, Mississippi, one Sunday night on the power of the name of Jesus. A visiting woman in a wheelchair came forward for prayer. She had suffered a stroke, and her doctor said she would never walk again. As we prayed for her, she slowly rose out of her wheelchair with some help and took a few halting steps. She was overjoyed, but that was just the beginning. Every day she grew progressively better, until eventually she regained her full ability to walk. The doctor told her pastor, "She is a miracle."

While I was preaching in Cseteny, Hungary, in 1987, someone brought to the service a young woman who had been mentally handicapped from birth. As we prayed for her, we felt the power of God, but there was no visible change in her condition. From that day forward, however, she began to improve. By the time I returned in 1988, her progress was so dramatic that her family, who had been unbelievers, confessed it to be a miracle and became Christians.

Her family, who had been unbelievers, confessed it to be a miracle and became Christians.

At a weekend seminar and revival in Petrovac, Yugoslavia, in 1988, we prayed for a woman in the hospital. She recovered miraculously, came to church, and received the Holy Spirit the moment we laid hands on her.

In a prayer meeting at our church in Austin, Texas, in October 1995, God spoke to us through tongues and interpretation and promised healing. That night, my mother-in-law accepted that promise for her and was instantly healed of a serious back injury she had received in an automobile accident two years earlier.

A missionary to Asia contracted an incurable, deadly form of hepatitis and was forced to return home. His doctors told him he could never travel or live in Asia again. Over several months, as he attended our church, we and many others prayed for his healing. Miraculously, he began to improve, was restored to full health, and a few months later received confirmation from his doctors that he could resume his missionary work.

In 1997 a woman came to our church in Austin suffering from severe depression; she was seriously contemplating suicide and had taken some steps to fulfill this intention. God filled her with the Holy Spirit, healed her of the depression, and set her free from thoughts of suicide.

HEALING IN THE ATONEMENT

Healing is more prominent in Scripture than many of the other gifts, probably for several reasons: it is more visible, it ministers more directly to urgent human needs, and it is particularly effective in evangelism. It is closely associated with God's plan of salvation, which He designed to reverse all the consequences of sin. He created us as both physical and spiritual beings, and His ultimate purpose is to redeem us physically and spiritually.

Indeed, the Bible declares that Jesus Christ purchased our healing as part of the Atonement: "Surely He has borne our griefs and carried our sorrows; yet we esteemed Him stricken, smitten by God, and afflicted. But He was wounded for our transgressions, He was bruised for our iniquities; the chastisement for our peace was upon Him, and by His stripes we are healed" (Isaiah 53:4-5).

Many people argue that this healing is exclusively spiritual, but God's salvation is for the whole person. Matthew 8:16-17 explains that physical healing is a fulfillment of

Isaiah 53:5: "When evening had come, they brought to Him many who were demon-possessed. And He cast out the spirits with a word, and healed all who were sick, that it might be fulfilled which was spoken by Isaiah the prophet, saying: 'He Himself took our infirmities and bore our sicknesses.'"

What Jesus did for the early church He will do for the church today.

"Jesus Christ is the same yesterday, today, and forever" (Hebrews 13:8). What He did for the early church He will do for the church today. He promised, "Most assuredly, I say to you, he who believes in Me, the works that I do he will do also; and greater works than these he will do, because I go to My Father. And whatever you ask in My name, that I will do, that the Father may be glorified in the Son. If you ask anything in My name, I will do it" (John 14:12-14).

When we say that healing is part of the Atonement, we mean that Christ's death, burial, and resurrection is the basis for our healing as well as our salvation. It does not mean that if we have faith to be saved then we will automatically be healed, or that if someone is not healed then he is not saved. We must realize that some of the benefits of the Atonement are immediate, while others are future.

Now is the day of salvation, in the sense of receiving

forgiveness of sins and the new birth, and everyone can enjoy these benefits immediately. But other aspects of our salvation are yet to come. We are still awaiting the redemption of the body in the ultimate sense of glorification. (See Romans 8:23; Philippians 3:20-21.) While some healing is available in this life, complete healing will come in the resurrection. Whatever we do not receive now, we will receive then. But Christ's sacrifice is the basis for all that we receive, both now and in eternity.

When we understand that healing does not come just by a whim but Christ has purchased it for us, we can pray for healing with great confidence. We will discuss reasons why we do not always receive instantaneous healing, but these reasons should not inhibit us from claiming God's promises. We should expect healing as the general will of God, without losing faith if it does not come in the time and manner that we expect. Even if we die while waiting for healing, we have not been defeated, because we will receive a glorified, immortal body in the resurrection.

PROGRESSIVE HEALING

Sometimes healing comes instantly; sometimes it is gradual or progressive. The human body has a built-in healing mechanism. When we cut a finger, it will normally heal of its own accord if we keep it clean and free from infection. Since God designed our bodies with their wonderful ability to recover, we can say in a general sense that all healing is of God. A surgeon does not actually heal the body but corrects a problem so that the body can heal itself. Similarly, God may sometimes simply remove whatever is preventing the body from healing itself and then let it resume its normal function. In such a case, the healing will be gradual but still of God.

Even in the Bible some healings were gradual.

Most scriptural accounts of healing describe instantaneous healing, for these cases are the most notable, and we certainly should expect such occurrences. Nevertheless, even in the Bible some healings were gradual. When ten lepers asked Jesus for mercy, He told them to show themselves to the priests, and as they went they were healed (Luke 17:12-14). While their healing came quickly, it was not evident when they asked or while they were with Jesus, but it became evident later.

Once, when Jesus healed a blind man, He had to give the man a second touch (Mark 8:22-25). After the first touch the man could see people as trees walking, but after the second touch he could see all things clearly. Perhaps the process was necessary to increase the man's faith. In any case, this account reveals that someone may receive partial healing and need continued faith and patience for full healing.

The Bible also reveals that some New Testament Christians suffered from sickness for a time without receiving immediate healing. Paul wrote about a preacher of the gospel who was seriously ill for a long time: "Yet I considered it necessary to send to you Epaphroditus, my brother, fellow worker, and fellow soldier, but your messenger and the one who ministered to my need; since he was longing for you all, and was distressed because you had heard that he was sick. For indeed he was sick almost unto death; but God had mercy on him, and not only on him but on me also, lest I should have sorrow upon sorrow" (Philippians 2:25-27). Paul also mentioned another preacher who was sick: "Erastus stayed in Corinth, but Trophimus I have left in Miletus sick" (II Timothy 4:20).

Someone may receive partial healing and need continued faith and patience for full healing.

Finally, another minister, Timothy, had chronic illnesses due to a weak constitution. Paul advised him, "No longer drink only water, but use a little wine for your stomach's sake and your frequent infirmities" (I Timothy 5:23). Apparently, Paul recommended that he drink nutritious grape juice instead of merely water, which could have been unsanitary. In any case, he showed that, while Christians always trust God for healing and strength, they should follow principles of good nutrition and health care.

These passages do not blame sick believers for their illnesses but demonstrate that it is not unusual for Christians to become sick. We still have a mortal body and live in a fallen world, and we are not immune from the diseases, trials, and tribulations of everyday life. We should not view sickness as a defeat but as an opportunity for healing. Whether we receive instant or gradual healing, we give God the glory. If we suffer for a time before recovery, then we learn patience, trust, and other lessons from God. If we die in faith, as everyone will one day (unless the Rapture occurs first), we still have our eternal reward.

THE ROLE OF DOCTORS AND MEDICINE

Whether in sickness or in health, we should place our trust in God. When ill, we should look first, foremost, and continually to God for healing and deliverance. We must not put our faith in doctors or medicine instead of God, but it is not wrong to consult doctors or to take medicine. Paul described his coworker Luke as "the beloved physician" without any hint of condemnation for his profession (Colossians 4:14).

Doctors perform many valuable services. They educate us in principles of good health such as proper diet, exercise, and hygiene in order to prevent illnesses and epidemics. They alert us to dangers and problems, and when the body fails to function properly, they help put it back on the course God intended. Their knowledge and skill ultimately come from God, and the medicines they use have their origin in herbs, vitamins, minerals, and other substances that God created for our use. Often, medication simply substitutes for something that the body normally provides. In time of sickness we should pray for healing, but if complete healing does not come immediately, there is nothing wrong with using various aids to help the body, including doctors, medication, casts, crutches, and wheelchairs.

Of course, we must evaluate all medical treatments carefully, seeking the will and wisdom of God in everything. Our society overuses medication; the tendency is to think there is a pill for every problem. But we need to be aware of the limitations, side effects, and dangers of various medications and procedures. Moreover, some treatments may not be appropriate for the child of God. A doctor once recommended that my mother undergo hypnosis for pain, but she rejected that option, feeling it would subject her mind to an unwarranted degree of control by an unbeliever.

Sometimes people feel that God has healed them and they no longer need medical treatment. If God has spoken to them, they should stand on His promise. Moreover, if God has healed them, they will be able to obtain verification from the doctors. They should accept healing from God, but they should not discontinue medical treatment as a means of proving their faith and thereby "requiring" God to heal them.

FAITH WHEN DELIVERANCE OR HEALING DOES NOT COME

Our faith must rest in God Himself, not in a theology of instantaneous deliverance or healing. Sometimes God does not answer our prayers in the way we desire or expect; nevertheless we trust in Him. Job affirmed, "Though He slay me, yet will I trust Him" (Job 13:15). God is not the author of sicknesses or hardships—the sin of the human race has brought these things into the world—but He does allow them to come our way.

Our faith must rest in God Himself.

We should not become discouraged when trials come, but we should seek the will of God in them. James 1:2-4 says, "My brethren, count it all joy when you fall into various trials, knowing that the testing of your faith produces patience. But let patience have its perfect work, that you may be perfect and complete, lacking nothing." God does not prevent trials, but He always provides grace to sustain and deliver us in time of trial: "No temptation has overtaken you except such as is common to man; but God is faithful, who will not allow you to be tempted beyond what you are able, but with the temptation will also make the way of escape, that you may be able to bear it" (I Corinthians 10:13).

Sometimes God delivers us miraculously from a trial, but sometimes He allows us to go through a trial. For example, King Herod arrested two apostles, Peter and James. God miraculously delivered Peter from prison, but He did not stop James from being beheaded. The same church prayed for both men. We cannot blame the church or James for lack of faith, but we must recognize that both men lived and died in faith and in the will of God.

When Paul was arrested in Jerusalem, he did not obtain a miraculous deliverance like that of Peter, so he availed himself of all legal protections and appeals. He could have become bitter because God did not deliver him, or he could have given up all attempts to extricate himself on the theory that he should not fight against the apparent will of God. Both choices would have been wrong, however. It was God's will for him to endure patiently, continuing to pray, work for release, and do whatever he could to further the gospel. In the end, Paul was executed, but in the meantime he was able to witness to various governmental leaders, including the Roman emperor, and he was able to write letters that are part of the New Testament today. God had a purpose in Paul's trials that was greater than Paul could realize at the time; he simply had to live by faith.

Sometimes God delivers us miraculously from a trial, but sometimes He allows us to go through a trial.

Paul also battled "a thorn in the flesh," which was "a messenger of Satan to buffet me." It was the satanic opposition he encountered everywhere he went to preach the gospel. Some think it involved a physical problem; in any case it was not of God. Three times Paul prayed for deliverance, but God did not answer the prayer as he wished. Instead, God told him, "My grace is sufficient for you, for My strength is made perfect in weakness." (See II Corinthians 12:7-9.)

The principles we have discussed hold true for physical illness. Romans 8:28 tells us, "And we know that all things work together for good to those who love God, to those who are the called according to His purpose." We may not be able to identify a particular good that comes from each negative event, but when we consider our life as a whole we will be able to see that God has worked all things together—both positive and negative experiences—for our ultimate good. In sickness, then, we must continue to love God, do His will, and trust Him. If something in our life is not pleasing to Him, we should repent and correct our ways. We should pray and believe for divine healing, but if we are sick for a time we should use whatever means He has made available to us for alleviation of suffering and progress toward recovery.

An aunt of mine was diagnosed with cancer while in her forties. She had great faith in God, and several times in prayer she believed God had miraculously healed her. From all indications, if anyone had faith she did, and those closest to her testified of her great faith. During her trial God spoke to her through tongues and interpretation, promising that she would live to see the third generation of her family. At the time, two of her four children were married, but she had no grandchildren. The family took this promise to mean she would be healed, but it was not to be. Shortly after the prophetic word, both her daughter and daughter-in-law found that they were expecting a baby. A few months after the two grandchildren were born, my aunt passed away. The family could not explain why God allowed this event, but they still trusted Him. As one positive development from this severe trial, another aunt of mine was so inspired by this example of faithfulness unto death that she renewed her own walk with God.

Faith is not only manifested in miraculous deliverance.

Faith is not only manifested in miraculous deliverance; faith can be equally seen in patient endurance through trials. Hebrews 11 lists many heroes of faith: some received miracles through faith while others died in faith without receiving a miracle. All obtained the commendation of God and serve as role models for us. The three young Hebrews in Babylon fully expected a miraculous deliverance, but if God did not deliver them they were still committed to serving Him. They told Nebuchadnezzar, "Our God whom we serve is able to deliver us from the burning fiery furnace, and He will deliver us from your hand, O king. But if not, let it be known to you, O king, that we do not serve your gods, nor will we worship the gold image which you have set up" (Daniel 3:17-18).

Some people erroneously teach that divine healing will inevitably come if only people have enough faith, make the correct confession, or follow a certain procedure. But God is sovereign; we cannot comprehend Him much less manipulate or dictate to Him. By definition, faith always retains an element of mystery, of the unknown, of trust despite a lack of understanding. We can never reduce it to a simplistic, ironclad formula.

A former student of mine became acquainted with a charismatic church in Texas that strongly taught the doctrine of positive confession: if a person confessed his healing with complete faith he would inevitably be healed. A board member of the church was diagnosed with incurable cancer. The church prayed, confessed, bound together, and named and claimed victory. The man did not receive healing but continued to deteriorate. Finally, the leaders of the church informed him that their faith was strong; the reason he was not healed was his own lack of faith. He rejected this conclusion and was forced to leave the church. When he needed encouragement the most, this doctrine was used to attack him. In the end, however, after leaving that church he did receive a miraculous healing.

WHY HEALING SOMETIMES DOES NOT COME

Why do some people not receive healing? We can identify several possible reasons.

1. *Lack of faith.* As we have discussed, many people who have faith are not healed. Nevertheless, as we shall see in chapter 10, faith is a key to receiving healing from God. When we seek healing, we must focus our faith on

the Lord and His promises. Probably the greatest reason we do not see more miraculous healings from God in our world today is lack of faith. Although Jesus was a great healer and miracle worker, when He returned to Nazareth for a visit most people did not accept His ministry because they thought they knew Him and His family so well. Consequently, "He did not do many mighty works there because of their unbelief" (Matthew 13:58).

2. *Our own actions.* When healing does not come, we should not only examine our faith but we should examine our lifestyle, actions, and environment. Many times, sickness results from our own inadvertent or deliberate actions.

Sometimes, but not always, sickness is the result of sin. After healing a bedridden man at the Pool of Bethesda, Jesus told him, "See, you have been made well. Sin no more, lest a worse thing come upon you" (John 5:14). Paul explained that irreverence for the Lord's Supper could have serious physical consequences: "He who eats and drinks in an unworthy manner eats and drinks judgment to himself, not discerning the Lord's body. For this reason many are weak and sick among you, and many sleep" (I Corinthians 11:29-30). God may allow chastisement to come to us in the form of sickness because of a wrong we have committed against someone else, and in such cases we need to repent and confess that wrong in order to be healed. (See James 5:16.)

There are many examples in which a violation of God's will results in a specific sickness or disease. Drinking alcoholic beverages can cause cirrhosis of the liver, smoking can cause emphysema and lung cancer, fornication and adultery can result in venereal diseases and AIDS, and harboring hatred and bitterness can contribute to a variety of stress-related illnesses. Persistent rebellion against God can lead to mental and emotional breakdown.

Most sicknesses and handicaps are not the direct result of an individual's sin, however. When the disciples saw a blind man, they assumed his condition was due to someone's sin, but Jesus corrected them. "And His disciples asked Him, saying, 'Rabbi, who sinned, this man or his parents, that he was born blind?' Jesus answered, 'Neither this man nor his parents sinned, but that the works of God should be revealed in him'" (John 9:2-3). Job's friends tried to blame his condition on sin in his life, but he rejected their conclusion, and God ultimately vindicated him.

*We should not judge
others who are sick.*

Sickness can also result from an unhealthy diet, poor hygiene, lack of exercise, stress, lack of rest, and environmental causes. While we can seek God's help in these situations, it would be presumptuous to pray for divine healing without attempting to correct the factors that lie in our control. We cannot blame God if we become sick due to our own actions, nor can we say God has failed if

He does not heal us instantly in such cases.

We should not judge others who are sick, but we should examine ourselves to see if God is trying to chasten or teach us through an illness. Our violation of a physical or spiritual law could be the cause, and if so we need to correct our ways. If, after examining ourselves prayerfully, we do not see such a cause, we should not live in guilt and condemnation but should continue to walk by faith.

3. *The general versus specific will of God.* While the Bible gives a general promise of healing to the church, it may not be the will of God to heal instantly in a specific case. All prayers must be subject to the will of God. Jesus taught us to pray, "Your kingdom come. Your will be done on earth as it is in heaven" (Matthew 6:10). He Himself prayed in the Garden of Gethsemane, "Father, if it is Your will, remove this cup away from Me; nevertheless not My will, but Yours, be done" (Luke 22:42). God promises to hear and grant "whatever we ask," but this promise is predicated upon our asking "according to His will" (I John 5:14-15).

James 5:14-16 instructs us to pray for the sick; thus it is always God will for us to do so. We should pray for a sick person's healing, and we have assurance that God will hear and answer this prayer—but in His manner and time, not necessarily ours. He may heal instantly, He may begin a gradual process of healing, He may use what we consider "natural" means, He may heal later, He may give grace through a time of sickness, or He may allow the person to die in faith and receive the answer in the resurrection.

There can be many reasons why God does not heal instantly; some we can discern, while others are known only to the sovereign mind of God. For instance, instead of relieving our temporary symptoms by a miraculous healing, the Lord may allow us to remain sick for a time so that we will correct the root causes of our sickness.

Pain is important in this regard. While none of us likes pain, it is important to listen to our bodies when we have pain. Instead of ignoring a chronic ache, we should seek to understand the cause. People with leprosy gradually lose feeling in their extremities. They do not feel pain when they injure a foot or finger, for instance, and will go for hours or days without correcting a serious problem. As a result, their bodies gradually suffer irreparable damage. Thus it can be a blessing for God not to remove pain immediately but to allow it to help us.

Sometimes God may use an illness to accomplish a specific purpose in our lives.

Sometimes God may use an illness to accomplish a specific purpose in our lives or the lives of others. The blind man in John 9 lived with his condition for many years until God's time for a miracle, and Jesus explained that it was God's purpose to reveal His works through this man. Many times Jesus must have passed the lame man who sat at the Temple gate for years, but he was not healed until Peter and John prayed for him in Acts 3.

After my family suffered a terrible head-on collision in 1963, my parents had to stay in a hospital for many weeks. My mother came within a hair's breadth of death with a broken neck and a brain concussion. My father's nose and both arms were broken. The accident delayed our going to Korea for a year. From our perspective the suffering and loss of time did not seem understandable, but at least one good thing came out of this ordeal. My father had the opportunity to witness to a nurse about salvation. She repented in the hospital room where he lay incapacitated. She then went to church, was baptized in Jesus' name, received the Holy Spirit, and is still living for God many years later.

Finally, Ecclesiastes 3:2 tells us there is "a time to die." At some point, God does not heal miraculously but allows us to pass from this life to the next. Even in cases where life seems to be cut short unfairly, we must trust God's judgment. Only He knows what could have happened had the person lived longer, and only He knows what will happen as a result of the person's death.

From the perspective of eternity, we will see all things clearly. The sufferings of this life will seem light, and all earthly lives will seem but a moment.

In conclusion, we should pray for healing unless God impresses us otherwise. We should not use any of the factors just discussed as an excuse not to believe God's promises of healing. We must pray in faith and live in faith. When we do, we will observe and experience God's miraculous healing power on a regular basis. Most of all, we will realize that God does not always act as we wish or expect but works all things together for our good.

CHAPTER TEN

FAITH FOR HEALING

Divine healing is a sign that follows believers. Jesus promised, "And these signs will follow those who believe: In My name they will cast out demons; they will speak with new tongues; they will take up serpents; and if they drink anything deadly, it will by no means hurt them; they will lay hands on the sick, and they will recover" (Mark 16:17-18). All believers—not just apostles, prophets, or preachers—can overcome Satan's power, speak in tongues, enjoy divine protection, and pray successfully for divine healing of the sick.

Some people who do not believe in miracles today try to discredit the teaching of Mark 16:17-18 by challenging believers to pick up poisonous snakes or drink poison. This passage does not endorse such practices, however. It does not instruct us to tempt God, but it affirms that we can have faith for divine protection from danger. When the devil tempted Jesus, he quoted a promise of divine protection from the Psalms and challenged Jesus to jump from the pinnacle of the Temple. Jesus replied, quoting from Deuteronomy, "You shall not tempt the LORD your God" (Luke 4:12). If we deliberately put ourselves in harm's way to test God or to exalt self, then we cannot rely on God's promise of protection.

Since I Corinthians 12 lists healing among the supernatural spiritual gifts that God gives at different times to different individuals but not to everyone, we can conclude that not everyone will receive healing every time we pray. Even so, Mark 16:17-18 tells us that all believers should expect to see healings in response to their prayers.

We are to pray for all believers who are sick and it is the general will of God to heal them.

In addition, James 5:14-15 tells us that we are to pray for all believers who are sick and that it is the general will of God to heal them: "Is anyone among you sick? Let him call for the elders of the church, and let them pray over him, anointing him with oil in the name of the Lord. And the prayer of faith will save the sick, and the Lord will raise him up. And if he has committed sins, he will be forgiven." The word "sick" comes from the Greek *astheneo*, which appears many times in the Gospels with reference to those who are physically ill. The KJV variously translates it as "diseased, impotent, sick, weak." The Lord is the one who raises up the sick, and He responds to "the prayer of faith."

Both Mark 16:17-18 and James 5:14-15 instruct us that, as a general principle, we should expect sick people to be healed when we pray, and both emphasize the importance of faith in receiving healing. Let us examine the role of faith further.

THE VITAL ROLE OF FAITH

There are numerous accounts of healing in the Gospels and Acts, and in most of them faith is prominent. While God is sovereign and can perform a miracle anytime He chooses, it is obvious that He responds to faith. The person who needs healing should have faith; if he cannot, then others can have faith on his behalf. Here are some scriptural examples that demonstrate the necessity of faith for healing:

• "Then He touched their eyes, saying, 'According to your faith let it be to you'" (Matthew 9:29).

• "And He did not do many mighty works there because of their unbelief" (Matthew 13:58).

• "When Jesus saw their faith, He said to the paralytic, 'Son, your sins are forgiven you'" (Mark 2:5). This man was unable to come to Jesus by his own power, but friends of his let him down through the roof of the house where Jesus was teaching a multitude. As a result of their faith, he was able to meet the Lord, who granted both forgiveness (which required repentance and faith on his part) and healing. The man and his friends had faith together.

• "Then Jesus answered and said to her, 'O woman,

great is your faith! Let it be to you as you desire.' And her daughter was healed from that very hour" (Matthew 15:28). Jesus healed the daughter because of the faith of the mother.

• "And He said to her, 'Daughter, your faith has made you well. Go in peace, and be healed of your affliction'" (Mark 5:34).

• "As soon as Jesus heard the word that was spoken, He said to the ruler of the synagogue, 'Do not be afraid; only believe'" (Mark 5:36).

• "Jesus said to him, 'If you can believe, all things are possible to him who believes.' Immediately the father of the child cried out and said with tears, 'Lord, I believe; help my unbelief!'" (Mark 9:23-24). This man believed, but he recognized that doubts were assailing him and asked for divine help to overcome them. The Lord responded to this prayer by healing the man's son.

• "Then Jesus said to him, 'Go your way; your faith has made you well.' And immediately he received his sight and followed Jesus on the road" (Mark 10:52).

• "And in Lystra a certain man without strength in his feet was sitting, a cripple from his mother's womb, who had never walked. This man heard Paul speaking. Paul, observing him intently and seeing that he had faith to be healed, said with a loud voice, 'Stand up straight on your feet!' And he leaped and walked" (Acts 14:8-10). It does not seem that the apostles prayed for every sick or handicapped person in every city. Rather, they looked for people who had faith. On this occasion, God showed Paul that this man had faith to be healed. Paul spoke boldly because he perceived the man's faith, and the man was healed.

Jesus healed everyone who came to Him in faith; for instance, in Matthew 8:16 He "healed all that were sick." As we have seen, however, even He did not heal every sick person within His reach, for He did not do many miracles in Nazareth due to the people's unbelief. His example indicates that we should not go into every nursing home and hospital to pray indiscriminately for everyone, but we need to proclaim the message of healing and pray for those who respond in faith.

Jesus healed everyone who came to Him in faith.

The apostles, eyewitnesses of Jesus' miraculous ministry, had great faith when it was time for their own ministry. On at least some occasions, everyone they prayed for was healed also. Acts 5:14-16 records, "And believers were increasingly added to the Lord, multitudes of both men and women, so that they brought the sick out into the streets and laid them on beds and couches, that at least the shadow of Peter passing by might fall on some of them. Also a multitude gathered from the surrounding cities to Jerusalem, bringing sick people and those who were tormented by unclean spirits, and they were all healed." Peter's shadow did not have magical power, but the people's faith rose in his presence in response to his obvious relationship with God, and God in turn responded to their faith. Nevertheless, as we saw in chapter 9, not everyone in the early church received instantaneous healing.

We should pray and believe for a healing ministry like that of the apostles, and thus we should expect numerous healings, sometimes for a multitude at one time. If we do, the church will see more healings today than in the three years of Christ's earthly ministry, in fulfillment of His promise of "greater works" (John 14:12). At the same time, we must recognize the uniqueness of the ministry of Jesus: He had perfect insight into the faith of people and the will of God for them, He had all power and authority as God manifested in flesh, and He used healings as a means of establishing His messianic identity. (See Matthew 8:16-17; 28:18; John 2:24-25.) Thus only His healing ministry stands as an example of perfection.

CALLING ON THE NAME OF JESUS

Not only must we have faith, but it is necessary to have faith in Jesus Christ, the one who purchased our healing by the stripes on His back at the Atonement. The power of faith does not rest in our mental belief or verbal confession, but in the object of our faith. We will receive healing only if the one we call upon has the power to heal, and Jesus is the One who has all power.

For this reason, the Bible instructs us to pray for healing in the name of Jesus. His name is not a magical formula, but when we invoke His name in faith we place our faith in the person and work of Jesus Christ, and we demonstrate that faith to all by obeying His Word. Here are some scriptural statements of the importance of praying in the name of Jesus:

The Bible instructs us to pray for healing in the name of Jesus.

• "And these signs will follow those who believe: In My name they will cast out demons; they will speak with new tongues; they will take up serpents; and if they drink anything deadly, it will by no means hurt them; they will lay hands on the sick, and they will recover" (Mark 16:17-18). All these works take place in the name of Jesus.

• Jesus said, "If you ask anything in My name, I will do it" (John 14:14).

• "Is anyone among you sick? Let him call for the elders of the church, and let them pray over him, anointing him with oil in the name of the Lord" (James 5:14).

• "Then Peter said, 'Silver and gold I do not have, but what I do have I give you: In the name of Jesus Christ of Nazareth, rise up and walk'" (Acts 3:6). This verse records what Peter said when the lame man at the Temple was healed.

• "And His name, through faith in His name, has made this man strong, whom you see and know" (Acts 3:16). Here Peter explained to the multitude how the lame man was healed.

• "And when they had set them in the midst, they asked, 'By what power or by what name have you done this?' . . . 'Let it be known to you all, and to all the people of Israel, that by the name of Jesus Christ of Nazareth, whom you crucified, whom God raised from the dead, by Him this man stands here before you whole. . . . Nor is there salvation in any other, for there is no other name under heaven given among men by which we must be saved'" (Acts 4:7, 10, 12). Here Peter explained to the Jewish religious leaders how the lame man was healed.

• "Now it came to pass, as Peter went through all parts of the country, that he also came down to the saints who dwelt in Lydda. There he found a certain man named Aeneas, who had been bedridden eight years and was paralyzed. And Peter said to him, 'Aeneas, Jesus the Christ heals you. Arise and make your bed.' Then he arose immediately. So all who dwelt at Lydda and Sharon saw him and turned to the Lord" (Acts 9:32-35).

• "But Paul, greatly annoyed, turned and said to the spirit, 'I command you in the name of Jesus Christ to come out of her.' And he came out that very hour" (Acts 16:18).

FOCUSING FAITH

It is not enough to believe generally that God can heal or even that He will heal eventually. Faith must act in the present to say, "I am receiving my healing now!" Jesus and the apostles often used symbolic acts to help people focus their faith to receive healing at a specific time. Here are some examples:

• "Then they brought to Him one who was deaf and had an impediment in his speech, and they begged Him to put His hand on him. And He took him aside from the multitude, and put His fingers in his ears, and He spat and touched his tongue. Then, looking up to heaven, He sighed, and said to him, 'Ephphatha,' that is, 'Be opened.' Immediately his ears were opened, and the impediment of his tongue was loosed, and he spoke plainly" (Mark 7:32-35).

Jesus and the apostles often used symbolic acts to help people focus their faith.

• "When He had said these things, He spat on the ground and made clay with the saliva; and He anointed the eyes of the blind man with the clay. And He said to him, 'Go, wash in the pool of Siloam.' . . . So he went and washed, and came back seeing" (John 9:6-7).

• "Now God worked unusual miracles by the hands of Paul, so that even handkerchiefs or aprons were brought from his body to the sick, and the diseases left them and the evil spirits went out of them" (Acts 19:11-12).

In these instances, we must not suppose that saliva, clay, or handkerchiefs were necessary for the healing. They were simply tools to focus the recipients' faith. When Jesus touched the tongue of the man with a speech impediment, the man realized that something was going to happen to his tongue at that moment. When the blind man washed the clay from his eyes in obedience to the command of Jesus, he expected something to happen right then.

When the prayer cloths from Paul were placed on sick people, they realized that a man of faith had prayed for them, and they joined their faith to his. This procedure, while not mandatory, is helpful when it is difficult for a sick person to meet with the elders of the church for prayer. They can pray over the cloth and send it to the sick person. He and his household can then join their prayers with those of the church and believe for healing.

In no case should we view the cloth as magical or indispensable, nor should we put our faith in an individual who has prayed over the cloth. Instead, we must realize that faith is the key, and the faith must be in Jesus Christ.

There are two symbolic actions that the Bible recommends when praying with the sick: anointing with oil and the laying on of hands. The primary purpose of both is to focus faith at a specific time. We will discuss the former now and the latter in chapter 11.

ANOINTING WITH OIL

James 5:14 instructs, "Is anyone among you sick? Let him call for the elders of the church, and let them pray over him, anointing him with oil in the name of the Lord." The elders (ministers, pastoral staff) are to anoint the sick with oil.

Some modern commentators say this verse speaks of medical treatment. In ancient times, medical techniques were limited, and people poured oil on sores or into wounds. But if this be the meaning of James 5, why should the elders act as physicians, and why should they use oil for every illness from headache to cancer? Throughout Scripture, men of God used oil for a symbolic anointing, and this meaning is the obvious one here.

We find a good example in Mark 6. There, Jesus sent out the twelve disciples to preach the gospel. He did not send them as physicians, but He gave them power to cast out demons and heal the sick. Mark 6:13 records, "And they cast out many demons, and anointed with oil many who were sick, and healed them."

Anointing with oil reminds everyone that healing comes by the power of the Holy Spirit.

In numerous instances throughout Scripture, oil is symbolic of the Holy Spirit. In the Old Testament, prophets, priests, and kings were anointed with oil to signify the anointing of God upon them for the calling He had given them.

The New Testament refers to this symbolism: "But you have an anointing from the Holy One, and you know all things. . . . But the anointing which you have received from Him abides in you, and you do not need that anyone teach you; but as the same anointing teaches you concerning all things, and is true, and is not a lie, and just as it has taught you, you will abide in Him" (I John 2:20, 27).

We have an "unction" (KJV) or an "anointing" (NKJV)

in our lives. The word "anointing" literally refers to oil being poured over someone, but here it speaks of the Holy Spirit that is poured out upon us.

Anointing with oil is not strictly necessary for healing; indeed the vast majority of biblical accounts of healing do not mention it. When the elders gather to pray over a sick believer, however, anointing with oil is recommended. It reminds everyone that healing does not come from the elders but by the power of the Holy Spirit. The anointing also serves to focus the faith of the recipient. The touch of the oil reminds him of God's promise and gives him a specific moment to believe for the touch of God.

FOR ALL BELIEVERS

Some modern theologians argue that the day of miracles is over and, in particular, that divine healing was only for the apostles to administer. When confronted with biblical examples to the contrary, they sometimes modify their theory to say that only the apostles or those ordained by them could pray for divine healing. But the scriptural passages we have discussed in chapter 9 and this chapter do not express such limitations; instead they proclaim the promise of healing for all believers. Let us note a few specific instances in the Book of Acts where people who were not apostles or prophets nevertheless were mightily used of God in various miracles.

• "And Stephen, full of faith and power, did great wonders and signs among the people" (Acts 6:8). Stephen was not one of the twelve apostles but one of the seven men chosen to handle food distribution, usually considered to be deacons.

• "And the multitudes with one accord heeded the things spoken by Philip, hearing and seeing the miracles which he did. For unclean spirits, crying with a loud voice, came out of many who were possessed; and many who were paralyzed and lame were healed" (Acts 8:6-7). This man was not the apostle Philip but, like Stephen, one of the seven deacons. Later the Bible speaks of him as an evangelist (Acts 21:8).

• "And Ananias went his way and entered the house; and laying his hands on him he said, 'Brother Saul, the Lord Jesus, who appeared to you on the road as you came, has sent me that you may receive your sight and be filled with the Holy Spirit.' Immediately there fell from his eyes something like scales, and he received his sight at once; and he arose and was baptized" (Acts 9:17-18). Ananias was a believer, perhaps an elder, in Damascus. He was not an apostle, and there is no evidence that he was ever ordained by an apostle.

These examples encourage us to believe God for the same manifestations today. The key to receiving divine healing is not the identity of the one who prays, but it is faith in Jesus Christ.

CHAPTER ELEVEN

THE LAYING ON
OF HANDS

As we noted in chapter 10, the Bible describes two important actions that can help focus faith to receive healing at a specific time: anointing with oil and laying on of hands. In this chapter we will discuss the significance of the latter.

Jesus promised, "And these signs will follow those who believe: In My name . . . they will lay hands on the sick, and they will recover" (Mark 16:17-18). Clearly, the laying on of hands is important for us to understand, especially if we want to see the promise of healing fulfilled in the church today.

Hebrews 6:1-2 identifies this practice as one of the foundational doctrines of the church: "Therefore, leaving the discussion of the elementary principles of Christ, let us go on to perfection, not laying again the foundation of repentance from dead works and of faith toward God, of the doctrine of baptisms, of laying on of hands, of resurrection of the dead, and of eternal judgment." Here "laying on of hands" refers to more than the simple act; it stands for a key doctrine. Apparently it represents the miraculous work of the Holy Spirit in the church, including the gifts of the Spirit, for in the Book of Acts the Holy Spirit commonly came with the laying on of hands.

IN THE OLD TESTAMENT

To understand this subject fully, we should start with its significance in the Old Testament. Patriarchs and prophets employed the laying on of hands in association with prayers of blessing, consecration, or ordination. When Jacob blessed Ephraim and Manasseh, he laid his hands on their heads (Genesis 48:14). When Moses ordained Joshua to be his successor, he laid his hands on him (Numbers 27:18-20; Deuteronomy 34:9).

On the Day of Atonement, the high priest used two goats to take away the sins of the nation. He sacrificed the first goat. Then he laid his hands on the second goat, confessed the sins of the people, and let this goat escape into the wilderness (Leviticus 16:21). This "scapegoat" symbolically carried away their sins, never to be seen again. Similarly, when an individual brought an animal sacrifice for his personal sin, he laid his hand on the animal's head (Leviticus 1:4; 4:4).

The common thread throughout these examples is the *symbolism of spiritual transfer*. Jacob transferred blessings to his grandchildren, Moses transferred authority and anointing to his successor, the high priest transferred sins from the people to the scapegoat, and the individual penitent transferred his sins to the sacrificial animal. These qualities did not flow magically or physically by means of the hands, but the laying on of hands represented what God would do spiritually and helped people to believe and accept the invisible act of God.

IN THE NEW TESTAMENT

In the New Testament the laying on of hands fulfilled the same purposes of symbolizing a spiritual transfer and inspiring faith. Jesus, the apostles, and early believers laid hands on people for blessing, healing, receiving the Holy Spirit, and consecration or ordination to service.

Laying on of hands did not occur in all such cases, however; thus it is not mandatory. (See, for example, Matthew 8:5-13; Acts 2:1-4; 10:44; 14:9-10.) As chapter 10 has already discussed, the key to receiving these benefits is faith, not a physical act as such, but the laying on of hands is a divinely appointed act that helps the recipient to focus faith to receive. Here are some New Testament examples:

Blessing

• "But Jesus said, 'Let the little children come to Me, and do not forbid them; for of such is the kingdom of heaven.' And He laid His hands on them and departed from there" (Matthew 19:14-15).

175

Healing

• "Now He could do no mighty work there, except that He laid His hands on a few sick people and healed them" (Mark 6:5). Jesus did not perform many miracles in Nazareth because of the people's unbelief, but when He found a few who believed He laid hands on them and healed them. Clearly, the laying on of hands is not effective apart from faith, but its value is in encouraging people to believe.

• "When the sun was setting, all those who had anyone sick with various diseases brought them to Him; and He laid His hands on every one of them and healed them" (Luke 4:40).

• "And it happened that the father of Publius lay sick of a fever and dysentery. Paul went in to him and prayed, and he laid his hands on him and healed him" (Acts 28:8).

Receiving the Holy Spirit

• "Then they laid hands on them, and they received the Holy Spirit" (Acts 8:17).

• "And when Paul had laid hands on them, the Holy Spirit came upon them, and they spoke with tongues and prophesied" (Acts 19:6).

Consecration or Ordination to Service

• "Whom they set before the apostles; and when they had prayed, they laid hands on them" (Acts 6:6). The apostles consecrated the seven men chosen to assist them in the distribution of food to needy saints; these men were apparently the first deacons.

• "Then, having fasted and prayed, and laid hands on them, they sent them away" (Acts 13:3). The elders at Antioch commissioned Paul and Barnabas as missionaries to the Gentiles. God called them, but the church recognized their calling and approved of their going at this time.

• "Do not neglect the gift that is in you, which was given to you by prophecy with the laying on of the hands of the eldership" (I Timothy 4:14). "Therefore I remind you to stir up the gift of God which is in you through the laying on of my hands" (II Timothy 1:6). Paul reminded Timothy of the gift he had received by the laying on of hands of the elders ("presbytery" in KJV), including himself. These two passages apparently refer to Timothy's ordination to ministry, at which time he received a prophecy as well. The gift here is probably a special anointing for ministry that he received from God at his ordination.

Based on these two references, some have supposed that in their discretion they could grant spiritual gifts to others through the laying on of hands or prophecy. But as we have already seen, I Corinthians 12 clearly states that God is the one who gives the gifts. God often works through the prayers of others, but He bestows spiritual gifts at His initiative and of His choosing, not theirs. A minister whom God has called and whose calling and qualifications the church has examined, should expect a special anointing and blessing when the elders ordain him by the laying on of hands.

• "Do not lay hands on anyone hastily, nor share in

177

other people's sins; keep yourself pure" (I Timothy 5:22). Timothy had the responsibility of organizing churches and appointing elders in them. Paul admonished him not to ordain people to the ministry too quickly, for if they were not qualified the one who ordained them would bear some responsibility for their failures.

PURPOSE AND SIGNIFICANCE

From these New Testament examples, we can identify several important purposes of the laying on of hands. *First*, the laying on of hands *symbolizes the transfer of blessings from God to us.* This practice is particularly helpful in praying for (1) blessing, (2) healing, (3) reception of the Holy Spirit, and (4) ordination to and anointing for service.

Second, the practice *signifies the joint work of God's Spirit and God's church* to bring these blessings to individuals. While God is sovereign and can perform these works without human hands, He wants to move through His church. While the blessings come from God, the church proclaims them and inspires people to have faith to receive them.

Third, it *represents submission to God and His church*. In everyday life, touching another person's head expresses intimacy or authority. A typical example is when an adult pats a child on the head. It is rare for one adult to touch another adult's head in public. When we allow elders to lay hands on our head in prayer, we demonstrate our submission to God and to godly leaders.

Prayer by itself acknowledges our need of God, but prayer with the laying on of hands acknowledges our need for both God and the church. Moreover, since the Bible teaches the laying on of hands, our acceptance of it is an act of obedient faith.

Fourth, the practice *represents consecration to God*. Humble submission over time leads to consecrated service. When those who seek the Holy Spirit receive the laying on of hands, they express not only their desire to receive the Spirit but also their new dedication to God. At an ordination service, the recipients not only seek the blessing and anointing of God upon their lives but they also signify their consecration to Him and His church.

> *The laying on of hands focuses people's faith to receive a promise from God at a particular time.*

Fifth, the laying on of hands is a powerful tool that *focuses people's faith to receive a promise from God at a particular time*. In Korea, I saw the laying on of hands used quite effectively in five-night revivals and camp meetings. Usually, on the first two or three nights the evangelist would emphasize repentance and surrender to God. On the last two or three nights he would build faith to receive. He would instruct the people that if they had prepared their hearts, then when they felt the hands of the ministry on their heads they should expect to receive the Holy Spirit, renewal, healing, or whatever they needed from God. After just a few minutes of prayer, people would receive their answers. Scores would be baptized with the Holy Spirit in a few days of revival services at local churches, and hundreds would be filled at camp meetings.

When I was a teenager in Korea, an American soldier visited one of our camp meetings. It was his first time in a Pentecostal service, and he wanted to receive what we had, so I explained repentance to him. Then I instructed, "When you have fully repented and surrendered everything to God, open your heart in faith. You will feel a sense of relief because of the confession of your sins. At that moment, begin thanking and praising God. As a sign that you have reached this point, raise your hands in worship. When I see you praising God, I will ask a Korean minister to lay hands on you as in the Book of Acts, and by faith you will receive the Holy Ghost." Sure enough, when we laid hands on him and prayed, he immediately began speaking in tongues.

In order for the laying on of hands to have maximum effect in building faith, we should not practice it indiscriminately or casually. It is most effective when people understand its significance and when they are ready to receive something specific from God. When I am praying with people to receive the Holy Spirit, I do not lay hands upon them until it appears that they have repented. If they are not familiar with this biblical practice, I explain it to them, sometimes briefly while they are still praying, and I urge them to believe at the moment they feel the hands touch them.

Because laying hands on people's heads symbolizes authority, in public settings it is usually best to reserve the exercise of this practice for people in spiritual leadership—the elders (ministry) or those they designate. In the biblical accounts, it was always spiritual leaders who laid hands on others. The recipient can more easily have confidence and faith if he knows that the person who lays hands on him is a recognized, proven leader. If a leader is not available, however, other believers can also lay hands on people who need an answer from God. (See Mark 16:17-18.) An option that helps communicate support and faith in a nonauthoritative manner is for a believer to lay a hand on a seeker's shoulder or arm when praying with him.

The laying on of hands figured prominently in the conversion of the first new person to be baptized in Jesus' name and filled with the Holy Spirit in our home missions church in Austin (1992). We gave her a home Bible study; then she visited a Sunday service and was deeply moved. Monday she stayed home from work repenting, and that night she came to our house to discuss some decisions she needed to make in order to live for God. I taught her further about repentance and the new birth, and we began to pray with her. She repented, the Spirit of God began to move on her, and after a short while she said, "I'm ready to be baptized." We took her to a private swimming pool, where I explained, "When you come up from the water, begin to praise the Lord for cleansing you from all your sins. I will lay hands on you, and at that moment expect to receive the Holy Spirit." When she came up out of the water, I laid hands on her and the Spirit fell. Immediately she began to speak in tongues as the Spirit gave the utterance.

In 1995 a man with bipolar disorder (manic-depression) came to our church. He was often suicidal and had been in and out of mental hospitals for years. After he repented earnestly, I prepared him for baptism. I instructed him that when I laid hands on him after baptism he should expect to receive the Holy Spirit with the sign of tongues. He replied, "I'm scared of that!" I told him not to worry but to believe and obey, and God would do the work. Matter-of-factly, he agreed. Because of his response and demeanor, I wondered if anything would happen, but as soon as he came up from the water and I laid hands on him, he began speaking in tongues as the Spirit gave utterance. Afterward his mental health improved dramatically, he was delivered from suicidal thoughts, and he was able to get his own apartment.

When we teach the significance of laying on of hands and prepare people to receive something from God at the laying on of hands, then we will see many marvelous healings and outpourings of the Spirit. When we obey the instructions of God's Word and focus our faith accordingly, we have the assurance that God will bestow His abundant blessings.

CHAPTER TWELVE

TONGUES AND INTERPRETATION

T he three *gifts of utterance* are "prophecy, . . . different kinds of tongues, . . . [and] the interpretation of tongues" (I Corinthians 12:10). By these gifts, God anoints people to communicate thoughts from His mind to the church. The speakers proclaim words of "edification and exhortation and comfort to men" (I Corinthians 14:3).

TONGUES

The Greek word for "tongue" in I Corinthians 12-14 is *glossa*. Like the word in English, it refers first to the organ of the body and then by extension to a spoken language. This passage clearly uses the word in the latter sense, as we see by the following examples: "He who speaks in a tongue does not speak to men but to God. . . . He who speaks in a tongue edifies himself" (I Corinthians 14:2, 4). The speaker does not know this language: "If I pray in a tongue, my spirit prays, but my understanding is unfruit-ful" (I Corinthians 14:14). Those who hear the speaker do not understand the language either (unless a foreigner or a bilingual person is present): "No one understands him" (I Corinthians 14:2).

We should note that there are "different kinds of tongues" (I Corinthians 12:10). One person may speak in one language, while another person may speak in a different language. The same person may also speak in more than one language. The language can be one that is used in the world today or one that is extinct. Presumably, it can also be a unique language specially created by God for one individual. I Corinthians 13:1 refers to "the tongues of men and of angels," which implies that someone could speak in an angelic tongue. Angels are spirit beings, and we do not know how they communicate with one another, but perhaps there is a heavenly language that we can imitate or approximate by human speech.

I have observed people speaking in tongues across the world—in Africa, Asia, Australia, Europe, and Latin America as well as the United States—and in all language groups and cultures the phenomenon is the same. I have heard singing in tongues, which is invariably beautiful. Sometimes an existing melody is borrowed; sometimes a new melody is created. Perhaps the most unusual tongues I have heard were a melodious, tonal language that sounded Oriental, spoken by a man in Jackson, Mississippi, and a sibilant, guttural language that sound-ed like a North American Indian tongue, spoken by a man in Houston, Texas.

At a prayer camp near Inchon, Korea, in 1972 I heard a Korean Methodist minister who was sitting next to me speak in tongues as he received the Holy Spirit. He repeated rapidly in English, with perfect diction and no discernible accent, "Jesus is coming very soon. Jesus is coming very soon." Afterwards I asked if he knew any English, but he did not. He had not understood anything he said; he was speaking in tongues in English.

The gift of tongues is the gift of a supernatural utterance in one or more languages unknown to the speaker.

We can define the gift of tongues as *the gift of a supernatural utterance in one or more languages unknown to the speaker.* We can identify three uses of tongues in the New Testament church: as the initial sign of the baptism of the Holy Spirit, in personal devotions, and as a public utterance to be interpreted. The physical and spiritual process is the same in each case, but the purpose and effect are different, as the following scriptural discussion will show.

INITIAL SIGN OF THE BAPTISM OF THE HOLY SPIRIT

First, speaking in tongues is *the initial sign that accompanies the baptism of the Holy Spirit.* The classic examples are the Jewish believers on the Day of Pentecost, the Gentile household of Cornelius, and the disciples of John at Ephesus. (See Acts 2:1-4; 10:44-48; 19:1-6.)

The Day of Pentecost illustrates that, while speaking in tongues is always unknown to the speakers, it is possible for a bystander to have natural human knowledge of the tongue and so to understand what is said. (See Acts 2:5-11.) For further discussion of this first use of tongues, as well as the nature of tongues in general, see chapter 9 of *The New Birth* by David K. Bernard.

Strictly speaking, we should not employ the term "gift of tongues" for this first use; it is rather a sign that accompanies the "gift of the Holy Spirit" (Acts 2:38). The gift of the Holy Spirit is for all believers (John 7:38-39; Acts 2:38-39; 11:15-17). By contrast, not everyone will exercise the gift of tongues for the edification of the body (I Corinthians 12:4-10, 30).

Speaking in tongues is for all believers.

Just as God grants all believers wisdom, knowledge, and faith, so speaking in tongues is for all believers. (See Mark 16:17.) Yet in each case there is a spiritual gift that goes beyond the everyday experience of all Christians and is used for special moments of need or benefit: the word of wisdom, the word of knowledge, the gift of faith, and the gift of tongues.

Some people deny the evidentiary role of tongues and further deny that everyone should seek the baptism of the Holy Spirit with this accompanying sign. They usually cite statements in I Corinthians 12-14 which indicate that not everyone will speak in tongues or that speaking in tongues must be regulated in certain ways. A comparison of Acts and I Corinthians quickly reveals, however, that they are confusing the uses of tongues.

I Corinthians was written to Spirit-filled believers; they had all been baptized with the Holy Spirit and had all spoken in tongues at least once. (See I Corinthians 6:11, 19; 12:13.) They obviously understood Paul's letter from that perspective. He did not teach that some of them would never speak in tongues, but he explained that not everyone would exercise the public gift of tongues in the life of the congregation, and when some did, they should follow certain guidelines.

On the Day of Pentecost, 120 believers spoke in tongues at the same time when they received the Holy Spirit. (See Acts 1:15; 2:1-4.) Likewise in Acts 10 the entire household of Cornelius spoke in tongues together, and in Acts 19 twelve disciples at Ephesus spoke in tongues together. Yet I Corinthians 14:27 says that in a public worship service believers should take turns speaking in tongues to the congregation, and only two or three people should give such messages. In the accounts in Acts no one interpreted the tongues or even tried to do so. Yet according to I Corinthians, if someone speaks in tongues in a service he should pray for the interpretation, and if there is none he should be quiet (I Corinthians 14:13, 28).

This contrast forces us to one of two conclusions: Either the apostolic church did not follow the inspired instructions of the apostle Paul regarding tongues, or the use of tongues in Acts is different from the use of tongues in I Corinthians. The former alternative is untenable, for it would undercut the unity of the church and the inspiration and authority of Scripture. Clearly, then, Acts and I Corinthians deal with two different situations. Acts records the role of tongues in the conversion of individuals, while I Corinthians provides guidelines for the continuing use of tongues in public meetings.

PERSONAL DEVOTION

The second use of tongues is *in personal devotion for private edification*. Several times I Corinthians 14 refers to this use of tongues and encourages it:

• "He who speaks in a tongue edifies himself. . . . I wish you all spoke with tongues" (I Corinthians 14:4-5). The Bible encourages all believers to speak in tongues, noting that this practice benefits and blesses the individual.

• "For if I pray in a tongue, my spirit prays, but my understanding is unfruitful. What is the result then? I will pray with the spirit, and I will also pray with the understanding. I will sing with the spirit, and I will also sing with the understanding" (I Corinthians 14:14-15). It is helpful to pray and sing in tongues and also to pray and sing in one's own language.

• "I thank my God I speak with tongues more than you all" (I Corinthians 14:18). Paul esteemed the devotional use of tongues to be of great value for him personally. By inspiring this evaluation as part of Scripture, God has urged all Christians to speak in tongues in their devotions.

It is desirable for everyone who has received the Holy Spirit to continue to speak in tongues throughout their lives.

These references indicate that it is desirable for everyone who has received the Holy Spirit to continue to speak in tongues throughout their lives. The implication of I Corinthians 12:30 that not everyone will speak in tongues seems directed toward the third use that we will discuss next, namely, public utterances to be interpreted. In practice, almost everyone who has received the Holy Spirit with the initial sign of tongues does continue to speak in tongues. Some speak in tongues frequently as part of their regular prayer, while others do so only at special times of renewing and great anointing.

A few do not continue to speak in tongues even though they continue to serve God. In many cases they received the Holy Spirit as a small child, and while living in the Spirit is a daily reality for them the actual experience of speaking in tongues has become remote.

Generally, if a Spirit-filled person is encouraged to pursue tongues for private devotion and to believe for this ongoing experience, he will speak in tongues again.

I received the Holy Spirit at the age of seven, but I did not speak in tongues again until I was a young adult. As a college student, I examined my personal beliefs and experience with God, and I began to seek God's will in this matter. I prayed often that God would grant me the liberty to speak in tongues in private devotion, for I concluded that it was His will for all believers to have this blessing. Gradually I began to break down reservations and doubt, to develop greater desire and faith, and to yield more fully to the Spirit.

We cannot judge our salvation or spirituality by how often we speak in tongues.

One Sunday night, as I prayed with several people at the altar, I began interceding for them with a heavy burden. Suddenly, without forethought or conscious desire, I began speaking in tongues. Over the next few weeks, I spoke in several different languages at various times of intercessory prayer. Today I do not speak in tongues every time I pray, nor do I try to do so, but I speak in tongues often, usually when praying for someone else or when caught up in a spirit of worship.

While speaking in tongues is valuable in private devotion, we cannot judge our salvation or spirituality by how often we speak in tongues. There is no biblical requirement that we must continue to speak in tongues after receiving the Holy Spirit, nor does the Bible tell us how often we should speak in tongues. If someone does not speak in tongues often, he should not feel guilty or doubt his salvation.

If a person formerly spoke in tongues more often, or if he feels that he should speak in tongues more often, he should examine himself. If the lack of speaking in tongues is due to a lack of dedication or fervent prayer, then he should renew his walk with God, not merely for the goal of speaking in tongues but to draw closer to God. If he has fallen away from God into a sinful lifestyle, he should repent and be renewed in the Spirit. In this case, speaking in tongues again is highly desirable as a confirmation of his renewed faith and surrender to God's Spirit as in times past.

As with other spiritual gifts, blessings, and manifestations, speaking in tongues itself does not prove that our doctrine, lifestyle, or relationship with God is correct. It simply demonstrates that at one point we received the Holy Spirit and that at present we have believed and yielded to God for the exercise of this particular manifestation. Instead of simply seeking tongues, we should emphasize fervent prayer, living by faith, obeying God's Word, and pursuing holiness. When we do, speaking in tongues will typically take its place in our lives as a means of personal edification, but it will not become a preoccupation or a panacea.

I taught a seminar in Hungary in 1987, the first one for the United Pentecostal Church in that country, not long before the fall of communism there. One of the topics was the spiritual gifts, and in attendance were two young Gypsy men whom I was asked to ordain to the ministry. During my teaching, one of the men stated that he had not spoken in tongues since he first received the Holy Spirit and confessed that he was greatly troubled as a result. I responded that he should not question his salvation or his experience but that speaking in tongues would be a great asset to his spiritual life and ministry and that God wanted to grant him this liberty. When it was time to pray, I encouraged him to have faith, and we laid hands on him for this purpose. Soon he began speaking in tongues by the power of God.

Just as the service was dismissed, the other young man acknowledged that he had the same problem. I reminded him of the experience of the first man and then gathered people around him also. As we prayed for him with the laying on of hands, he too began speaking in tongues.

PUBLIC UTTERANCE TO BE INTERPRETED

The third use of tongues is *as a public utterance to be interpreted for general edification.* God sometimes speaks to the church through the combined gifts of tongues and interpretation. The first gift, tongues, arrests the attention and reveals that God is trying to communicate with the audience. Because it is so miraculous and

spectacular, it is often quite effective in reaching nonbe-
lievers in attendance. The second gift, interpretation, discloses the actual message that God wishes to convey.
Here are two scriptural references to this use of tongues:

• "Even so you, since you are zealous for spiritual
gifts, let it be for the edification of the church that you
seek to excel. Therefore let him who speaks in a tongue
pray that he may interpret" (I Corinthians 14:12-13). The
purpose is to bless the entire congregation.

"If anyone speaks in a tongue, let there be two or at the most three."

• "If anyone speaks in a tongue, let there be two or at
the most three, each in turn, and let one interpret. But if
there is no interpreter, let him keep silent in church, and
let him speak to himself and to God" (I Corinthians 14:27-
28). These guidelines apply when someone speaks to the
church in tongues. If nobody interprets the words, the
speaker should not continue on and on. Instead, he
should speak to himself and to God. Either the tongue is
for his benefit alone, or else someone whom God wishes
to use for the interpretation has not fully yielded to Him.
In either case, continued speaking of tongues in public
will not accomplish God's intended purpose. In short,
when a speaker has the attention of the church, he should
speak in tongues only when there is an interpretation.

Some argue from this passage that no one should

ever speak in tongues in a church service without an interpretation, not even when everyone praises God or prays together. But in those times, everyone speaks for his own personal benefit, just as if he were alone. No one tries to capture the attention of the entire congregation, but everyone seeks personal edification, and thus speaking in tongues without interpretation is appropriate in this case. Verse 28 says as much: even in the congregation it is appropriate to speak in tongues without interpretation as a means of individual communication with God.

When no interpretation is forthcoming, we may think that the church has failed, but perhaps God has still accomplished a purpose by speaking to an individual or by helping someone to develop greater sensitivity to Him. On one unusual occasion in Baton Rouge, Louisiana, I witnessed a powerful utterance in tongues, but there was no interpretation. Yet that message touched two people in a very effective way.

First, an aunt of mine who was in the service had been told about the Pentecostal experience but had never heard anyone speak in tongues. She had often wondered whether speaking in tongues was real. That night she was convinced that it was, and she stated that God had performed this miracle for her benefit.

Second, a Lebanese student from Louisiana State University stated that the message was in his native language, Arabic. Initially he was angry at the person who had invited him to church, asking, "Why did you arrange for someone to speak to me in public and rebuke me for my sins?" Of course, neither the acquaintance who brought him nor the person who gave the message could speak Arabic or had any idea of the meaning of the utterance. God used this miracle to speak personally to the young man.

In the course of a service, the church can often sense when God is getting ready to speak by the gift of tongues. There is often a noticeable pause, a holy hush. The leader of the service will often realize what is about to take place. In one Sunday service in Austin, the time for preaching came, yet I felt that God was about to speak through tongues and interpretation, so I continued to lead the audience in worship. Soon my wife gave a public utterance in tongues, and someone else gave the interpretation. Before a Sunday night service in Austin, as I prayed in the prayer room, I felt that the Lord would speak to the congregation through the gifts of the Spirit. Near the close of that service, we had tongues, interpretation, and prophecy.

When God moves upon someone to speak to the church in tongues, he feels a strong anointing that he can readily distinguish from devotional tongues. He is able to speak with assurance and authority. Likewise, the church recognizes the utterance as a public message and not merely devotional tongues.

INTERPRETATION OF TONGUES

The Greek word translated "interpretation" is *hermeneia*, from which we get the English word *hermeneutics*, meaning principles of interpretation. To interpret means "to explain the meaning of" or "to translate orally." It means to give the sense of something, but it does not necessarily mean to translate word for word.

> *The interpretation of tongues is the gift of a supernatural ability to translate or explain the meaning of a public utterance in tongues.*

When someone speaks to the congregation in tongues, the gift of interpretation of tongues enables that person or someone else to proclaim the meaning of the utterance. "Let him who speaks in a tongue pray that he may interpret. . . . If anyone speaks in a tongue, let there be two or at the most three, each in turn, and let one interpret" (I Corinthians 14:13, 27). We can define the interpretation of tongues as *the gift of a supernatural ability to translate or explain the meaning of a public utterance in tongues.*

In many cases, it is impossible to translate one word in one language by one word in a second language, especially if the languages are not closely related. For some words there is no exact equivalent, and some words carry nuances or connotations that require explanation in another language.

For example, Greek has several words for the English

love: *agape* (selfless love), *phileo* (brotherly love), and *eros* (erotic love). The Korean word *kibun* refers to one's attitudes, feelings, disposition, and face (in the sense of saving face); no one English word can translate it. To describe a beautiful woman, English has "pretty, cute, beautiful, gorgeous, attractive, lovely, comely, stunning" and so on, all with varying shades of meaning, but Korean generally uses one word, *yehpun* or *ipun*. In each case, doing complete justice to the original language may require several words or even sentences in the second language.

Because of these differences, a short message can have a long interpretation, or vice versa. The literal translation of "Praise God!" in Korean is *hananim-keh chanyang-ul turimnida!* One reason why the Korean phrase is longer is that every Korean sentence has an untranslatable ending, which is equivalent to a spoken period or question mark and which indicates the relative status of the speaker and the hearer. The simple invitation "Come" is translated into Korean in various ways depending on whether the speaker is addressing an animal, child, or close friend (*wa*); a social equal (*osehyo*); a guest or superior (*oshipsheo*); or a king or God (*osheopsuhso*). In the latter two cases "Please come" is *oshegerul paramnida* and *oshegerul paramnahida*.

In addition, an interpretation often consists of an exposition or amplification of the original message. For example, Daniel gave Belshazzar the interpretation of the words God wrote on a wall. The words were "MENE, MENE, TEKEL, UPHARSIN." The literal translation is "numbered, numbered, weighed, divided." But Daniel gave the following interpretation: "This is the interpretation of each word. MENE: God has numbered your kingdom, and finished it; TEKEL: You have been weighed in the balances, and found wanting; PERES: Your kingdom has been divided, and given to the Medes and Persians" (Daniel 5:26-28).

God gives interpretations according to the speaker's mental ability, understanding, and expectation.

God gives interpretations according to the speaker's mental ability, understanding, and expectation. He will use the person's vocabulary, accent, and grammar to convey His message. If the person is schooled in the King James Version of the Bible and is prone to think of God's words in the Elizabethan English of that version, he may use words like *thee* and *thou*. If the speaker has not been conditioned in this manner, he will probably speak in modern English.

We should not discount a message because of a country accent, substandard grammar, a mispronounced word, or an archaic expression, but we should recognize that God has spoken His message through a human vessel. As an analogy, God has inspired all the books of the Bible and each word accurately reflects His message, yet the style, vocabulary, and grammar of the books reflect the personalities, backgrounds, and cultures of the various human authors.

Different people receive an interpretation in different ways. Some initially receive an idea, word, phrase, or even a picture. As they begin to speak in faith, God continues to impart His message and the words flow. Others explain that an interpretation comes much like speaking in tongues—with the cooperation of their tongue but without the advance understanding of their mind. They hear and comprehend the message along with everyone else.

Different people receive an interpretation in different ways.

I Corinthians 14 provides guidelines for the proper use of the gifts of tongues, interpretation, and prophecy in public worship. (See chapter 14 of this book.) While the true exercise of these gifts is of God, we should not claim infallibility for them. Each listener should judge whether a message is indeed of God, in part or in full, and how it applies to him personally. (See I Corinthians 14:29 and our discussion in chapter 13 of this book.) It is possible for the core message to be of God but for the human messenger to add his own fallible thoughts out of ignorance, excessive zeal, or pride. Some people become so proud of a vocal utterance that they assume all their thoughts and feelings at the time must be from the Lord. It is also possible for an utterance to be completely fleshly or even demonic.

As with tongues, I have observed many examples of interpretation of tongues around the world. It is particularly interesting to see tongues and interpretation at work in a language other than one's own. In Korea, I heard public tongues followed by interpretations in Korean, which I understood. In Italy, I heard a public tongue followed by an interpretation in Italian, which I did not understand; a man who knew both Italian and English translated the interpretation for me.

When I felt it was time to leave Jackson, Mississippi, in 1986, one of my main concerns was how my wife would respond. She was quite involved in the church and college, had many friends, and was very happy. I wanted her to feel the same leading that I felt. We prayed together for the will of God.

One day, she spoke to a lady in the church by telephone, and they began praying. This lady had no knowledge of what my wife and I were considering, but she spoke to my wife in tongues and interpretation. In essence she said, "God is getting ready to change the direction of your life. You don't understand now, but do not worry. Everything is going to be all right."

To my amazement, my wife became as eager to leave as I was, even though we did not know where we were going. The Lord performed a work simultaneously in our hearts, and He used tongues and interpretation to give a confirmation to my wife.

At a women's conference, my wife felt a strong burden to pray for an acquaintance. As she did, God spoke through her in tongues and interpretation, giving a message of encouragement for a time of trial. Although my wife knew nothing about the circumstances, the woman later confirmed that the words ministered to her needs and strengthened her at a crucial time.

In the fall of 1995, our young church in Austin faced an urgent situation. We had completely filled our rented building and needed to build our own facility if we wanted to grow. Over a two-year period, we had purchased property, developed architectural plans, obtained site and building permits, and secured financing. When we got ready to build, however, we found that we needed an extra one hundred thousand dollars because of certain special requirements and the construction boom occurring at that time. The situation seemed hopeless.

Instantly we felt a strong witness of the Spirit.

On Thursday, October 19, we had a prayer meeting at church. As I brought the service to a close, suddenly a young man burst forth with tongues and interpretation. The Lord told us: "You can't see healing, but I see healing. You can't see a miracle, but I see a miracle. You can't see a new building, but I see a new building."

Instantly we felt a strong witness of the Spirit. My mother-in-law was healed that night of a back injury. The following Tuesday night my wife's grandfather was brought back to life in the midst of an apparent stroke during our midweek service. The next Thursday, a major bank in Austin approved us for a fifteen-year building loan at the full amount we needed, with a lower interest rate that left our mortgage payment about the same as previously budgeted. Thus, within one week after the initial word from the Lord, we saw a healing, a miracle, and approval for our new building.

CHAPTER THIRTEEN

PROPHECY

The last vocal gift we will discuss is prophecy. The basic meaning of the Greek verb *propheteuo* is "to speak under inspiration" (Strong). Since God often revealed the future through the biblical prophets, the verb acquired the secondary meaning of "to foretell events." The English verb *prophesy*, which comes from the Greek, thus has two corresponding meanings: "to reveal by divine inspiration" and "to predict with certainty as if by divine inspiration." The English noun *prophecy* likewise means "an inspired utterance" or "a prediction of the future, made under divine inspiration." In other words prophecy can be "forthtelling or foretelling."

In a general sense, then, all speech anointed by God is prophecy. (See, for example, Ezekiel 37:4, 9.) It thus encompasses preaching, praising, and testifying. Prediction of the future is not a requirement. John's guide in Revelation told him, "I am your fellow servant, and of your brethren who have the testimony of Jesus. Worship

God! For the testimony of Jesus is the spirit of prophecy" (Revelation 19:10). In this sense all New Testament believers can prophesy (Joel 2:28; Acts 2:17), and prophecy is one of the service gifts (Romans 12:6).

I Corinthians 12:10 speaks of prophecy in a more restricted sense, however. Every believer should have an anointed testimony (Acts 1:8). Every preacher should preach the gospel with the anointing of the Spirit (I Corinthians 2:1-4). Yet according to I Corinthians 12:4-11, there is a specific gift of prophecy that not everyone exercises.

Prophecy is the gift of a supernatural utterance directly from God in the language of the speaker and hearers.

This gift is the equivalent of tongues followed by interpretation. "He who speaks in a tongue edifies himself, but he who prophesies edifies the church. I wish you all spoke with tongues, but even more that you prophesied; for he who prophesies is greater than he who speaks with tongues, unless indeed he interprets, that the church may receive edification" (I Corinthians 14:4-5). Thus the gift of prophecy is an utterance from God just as supernatural and specific as tongues and interpretation. We can define it as *the gift of a supernatural utterance directly from God in the language of the speaker and hearers.*

I Corinthians 14 calls the person who gives such an

utterance a "prophet." Again, this is a specialized, restricted use that applies strictly to the occasion. Someone who gives a prophecy is not necessarily a permanent prophet in terms of the fivefold ministry of Ephesians 4:11-16. As we saw in chapter 1, that passage refers to the office of a prophet. Of course, by definition we would expect someone who holds the office of a prophet to exercise the gift of prophecy at times.

The gift of prophecy can operate in several ways. A preacher may speak prophetically in the midst of a sermon. Someone in the congregation may address the congregation with a public utterance in the known language, much like the interpretation of tongues. Sometimes, God will anoint one individual to give a prophecy to another.

In a general sense, every anointed preacher prophesies when he preaches, but sometimes during the course of his message God will give him a direct word for the church or for certain individuals. At times the preacher may not fully realize what is happening, but at other times he may know that he has just spoken a specific word for someone. He may not know to whom it is directed, or God may reveal to him exactly who the intended recipient is. As the example of the high priest Caiaphas shows, it is possible for God to speak prophetically through someone without his fully realizing that fact or understanding the prophecy. (See John 11:49-52.)

BIBLICAL EXAMPLES

Acts 11:27-28 provides an example of public prophecy: "And in these days prophets came from Jerusalem to

Antioch. Then one of them, named Agabus, stood up and showed by the Spirit that there was going to be a great famine throughout all the world, which also happened in the days of Claudius Caesar." The church in Antioch responded to this prophecy by sending financial assistance to the believers in Judea, who were relatively poor.

The daughters of Philip the evangelist were well known for their prophecies. "Now this man had four virgin daughters who prophesied" (Acts 21:9-11). To merit such special mention, their ministry must have gone beyond the norm; probably they both preached and exercised the gift of prophecy.

Acts 21:10-11 offers an example of personal prophecy: "And as we stayed many days, a certain prophet named Agabus came down from Judea. When he had come to us, he took Paul's belt, bound his own hands and feet, and said, 'Thus says the Holy Spirit, "So shall the Jews at Jerusalem bind the man who owns this belt, and deliver him into the hands of the Gentiles.""'"

Previously, some disciples in Tyre had given Paul a similar message. "They told Paul through the Spirit not to go up to Jerusalem" (Acts 21:4). The Book of Acts reveals that Paul did go to Jerusalem, where he was arrested. From there he was put on trial, imprisoned for many months, and eventually sent to Rome for an appeal. At the close of Acts he was under house arrest. Tradition tells us he was ultimately executed in Rome. There is no indication that he missed the will of God in this matter, however. Indeed, he was firmly convinced that God wanted him to go to Jerusalem despite the consequences, and his coworkers finally accepted his decision as the will of God (Acts 21:13).

APPLYING A PROPHECY

The preceding story illustrates that, in the final analysis, only the recipients of a prophecy can decide what it means for them. They must discern whether a prophecy is of God, and if it is, how that prophecy applies to them. "Let two or three prophets speak, and let the others judge" (I Corinthians 14:29).

Only the recipients of a prophecy can decide what it means for them.

In Paul's case, the actual prophecy was not "You must not go to Jerusalem," but "If you go to Jerusalem, you will face persecution and arrest." Everyone else assumed this prophecy was God's way of telling Paul not to go, and they begged him not to, but Paul knew what God had already instructed him. He correctly concluded that the purpose of the prophecy was not to change his mind about going but to prepare him for what lay ahead and to encourage him that God would still be in control despite the adverse circumstances. The actual warning and prediction of danger came "through the Spirit," but not the conclusion that Paul should not go to Jerusalem.

As we discussed in chapter 1, the primary purpose of

the spiritual gifts is not to become an authority in some-one's life or to reveal the will of God that would other-wise remain unknown. Instead, they are part of the process of edification and confirmation. The one who prophesies must be careful not to let his own assumptions color the prophecy and not to jump to conclusions about the meaning of the prophecy for someone else. The one who receives a prophecy must be careful not to let it substitute for his own relationship with God and his own spiritual judgment.

For instance, if someone prophesies to an individual, "God is calling you to be a missionary to Brazil," the recipient must carefully evaluate what God is doing in his life. He should not act upon such a word unless it is the culmination of a process in which God has already dealt with him about the matter, or unless God confirms it through a further process of prayer and godly counsel. The exercise of a spiritual gift can plant a seed or serve as a confirmation, but it does not substitute for prayer, Bible study, and pastoral counsel in finding the will of God.

Prophecies are not infallible like the Bible.

As we noted about interpretations, prophecies are not infallible like the Bible. Of course, whatever is from God is true, but it is possible for even a well-intentioned person to let some of his own thinking intrude into a prophecy. He may elaborate on a thought that God gave, or he may misapply it. Once I heard a preacher proclaim publicly that God would heal a certain individual who was dying of a fatal disease. In my heart, I hoped and prayed that the word was true, but I did not feel assurance. After the sick person died, a leader explained the speaker's mistake in a charitable way: "We heard the voice of hope speak." The speaker had erred, not out of evil motives or influences but by following human emotions and desires.

CONTEMPORARY EXAMPLES

On many occasions, I have heard public prophecies from the Lord. Typically, they are messages of exhortation and encouragement that meet a special need or provide a special blessing in a particular service. One notable prophecy at a general conference warned that a newly commissioned missionary would face a great trial on the mission field, and the prophecy came to pass just as it was stated.

While I was teaching at Jackson College of Ministries, a visiting minister prayed with me after a service and gave a prophecy. The essence of it was that God would soon open a new door for me. Afterwards the minister asked, "Do you know what this prophecy is about? Has the Lord been dealing with you about something?" He did not presume to tell me how the prophecy applied, but he indicated that God would let me know.

At the time, some new opportunities had emerged, but I did not see a definite application of the prophecy.

Some months later, however, circumstances changed significantly, a new door opened, and I knew it was time for me to make a transition, although in a different way than I had previously considered. This prophecy helped to plant a seed in my mind so that I would be open to the new direction when it came. Not long afterwards, the Lord led us to the next phase of ministry. We moved to St. Louis, where I became the associate editor in the Editorial Division of the United Pentecostal Church International.

"The Lord wants to fill someone with the Holy Spirit here today."

In June 1989, not long before the fall of communism, I preached at a meeting of Apostolic ministers in Leningrad, Soviet Union (now St. Petersburg, Russia). Our missionary to eastern Europe had recently made the first face-to-face contact with Apostolic believers in Russia since the ministry of Andrew Urshan in 1916 before the communists took control. Then our missionary in Finland had taken a second trip to help set up this meeting. Now, I had come with him to meet with representatives from across the Soviet Union. I was to preach and teach, explain our beliefs, answer questions, and explore common ground with these believers.

As I began to preach on Sunday morning, I said, "The Lord wants to fill someone with the Holy Spirit here today." At the time, I did not view this statement as a prophecy but simply a feeling based on the general will of God. Unbeknown to me, however, these words presented quite a challenge to the audience. Due to years of secrecy, persecution, and isolation, they had developed the custom of praying for the Holy Spirit only in their homes. They conducted their public meetings in quiet, formal fashion, and when people wanted the Holy Spirit they made an appointment to meet them later. No one received the Holy Spirit at church.

After the preaching, the Lord began to move in a powerful way. People started praying and weeping, but the pastor sought to close the service. He selected someone to give the benediction, but that person began praying in the Spirit, and then a second person picked up the prayer in the same fervent fashion. Nevertheless, the pastor abruptly ended the service.

That afternoon, the men returned for teaching, questions, and discussion. One subject they asked about was divine healing, and I strongly affirmed that every local church should pray for healing. At the end, one of my questioners came to the front and requested prayer with the laying on of hands for healing. When he broke tradition in this manner, every other man in the building also came forward for prayer. The Spirit of God moved greatly, and soon one man received the Holy Spirit. He had come from Odessa, Ukraine—about one thousand miles away—in hopes of receiving this experience. At this, the host pastor stood up and said, with a change of attitude, "Our visitor from the West prophesied that someone would receive the Holy Spirit here today. Now God has fulfilled His prophetic word."

While my wife and I were in Nairobi, Kenya, on a missions trip in 1989, I received a call from my mother back in America. My sister Karen had awakened from a vivid dream that she felt was from the Lord. In the dream, I was physically attacked and my arms and legs cut off. Karen was so disturbed by this dream that she woke up sobbing, and my mother felt it was important to warn me of the possibility of impending danger. Perhaps we can consider the dream as a word of knowledge to my sister and the resulting message to me as a prophecy.

To my knowledge I did not encounter any danger in Kenya, but shortly after my return to America I faced surprising opposition from several people who misread or disagreed with a doctrinal article of mine.

Forewarned by this prophecy, I remained confident that God was in control.

I felt this strong opposition was the fulfillment of my sister's dream, and forewarned by this prophecy, I remained confident that God was in control. I explained my position to those who inquired about it but tried to leave the whole situation in the hands of the Lord. In the end, the entire situation was resolved harmoniously at the initiative of those who had opposed me.

On a number of occasions while I have been leading

a service, preaching, praying, or counseling, the Lord has prompted me to speak unplanned, unrehearsed words that applied to a certain situation or person. In some cases, I did not realize the extent to which God had spoken through me until afterwards. At other times, I immediately felt the words were specially anointed, and often an individual has later confirmed that the words were for him or her personally. My wife has had similar experiences in counseling and encouraging people.

One Sunday night in 1997, I was preaching a message in Austin on the grace of God. Near the close, I suddenly felt a powerful anointing to issue a strong warning against self-righteousness and judgment. The point was not in my plans, nor did it fit directly into my line of thought, but I instantly saw how I could tie it into my remarks. Later my wife, my mother-in-law, and a pastoral assistant each said they saw a transformation come over me as I spoke those few words. They concluded that the delivery was uncharacteristic of my style and personality but clearly of God.

As I spoke, I knew immediately to whom the words were directed, but I did not know if he would be receptive. The impression was so strong that I was concerned lest he accuse me of deliberately attacking him, although I did not directly address any identifiable situation. I knew he could react with anger and bitterness.

On the following Wednesday night, the man came to me in repentance. He had known immediately that the statement I made was from God and was for him personally. God dealt with him strongly for the next two days until he changed his attitude and behavior. The prophetic utterance defused a potentially serious problem and wrought a spiritual transformation.

CHAPTER FOURTEEN

I CORINTHIANS 14: THE VOCAL GIFTS IN PUBLIC WORSHIP

After introducing the spiritual gifts and teaching the importance of unity and love in the exercise of them, I Corinthians instructs us as to their proper use in public worship. It provides guidelines to eliminate confusion and to establish order so that the purpose of the spiritual gifts—to glorify Christ and to edify His body—can be fulfilled. I Corinthians 14 particularly addresses the three gifts of utterance—tongues, interpretation of tongues, and prophecy—because they have the greatest potential for misuse in a church service.

Some commentators disparage or deny the spiritual gifts today, and to bolster their case they point to some of the comments in I Corinthians 14 regarding the regulation of the vocal gifts. Unfortunately, those who have no spiritual experience in these matters are not qualified to comment. I Corinthians 2:12-14 explains, "Now we have received, not the spirit of the world, but the Spirit who is from God, that we might know the things that have been freely given to us by God. These things we also speak, not in words which man's wisdom teaches but which the Holy Spirit teaches, comparing spiritual things with spiritual. But the natural man does not receive the things of the Spirit of God, for they are foolishness to him; nor can he know them, because they are spiritually discerned." Only those who are filled with the Spirit will be fully able to comprehend and apply the teaching about spiritual gifts.

The solution to abuse is not disuse but proper use.

God inspired the apostle Paul to write I Corinthians 12-14 to correct abuses in the Corinthian church. The believers there zealously but immaturely exercised spiritual gifts without regard to the purpose for which God gave them. The result was chaos and confusion rather than edification. Paul's correction was not intended to diminish the spiritual gifts but to enhance their use and increase their effectiveness. The solution to abuse is not disuse but proper use. I Corinthians 14 addresses only those who exercise, or seek to exercise, the supernatural spiritual gifts.

Far from minimizing spiritual gifts, I Corinthians strongly encourages their continued use in a proper manner, as the following statements disclose:

• "The testimony of Christ was confirmed in you, so

that you come short in no gift" (1:6-7).

• "Earnestly desire the best gifts" (12:31).

• "Desire spiritual gifts, but especially that you may prophesy" (14:1).

• "I wish you all spoke with tongues, but even more that you prophesied" (14:5).

• "Since you are zealous for spiritual gifts, let it be for the edification of the church that you seek to excel" (14:12).

• "I thank my God I speak with tongues more than you all" (14:18).

• "How is it then, brethren? Whenever you come together, each of you has a psalm, has a teaching, has a tongue, has a revelation, has an interpretation. Let all things be done for edification" (14:26).

• "Desire earnestly to prophesy, and do not forbid to speak with tongues" (14:39).

PROPHECY AND TONGUES IN PUBLIC WORSHIP (I CORINTHIANS 14:1-14)

This passage commands us to seek after spiritual gifts and then explains the relative worth of the three vocal gifts in public worship.

"Pursue love, and desire spiritual gifts, but especially that you may prophesy" (verse 1).

The first half of the sentence puts the two preceding chapters into perspective: we must pursue love first, and having done so, we are to desire spiritual gifts. Then the verse tells us that prophecy is especially desirable in public meetings.

"For he who speaks in a tongue does not speak to men but to God, for no one understands him; however, in the spirit he speaks mysteries. But he who prophesies speaks edification and exhortation and comfort to men. He who speaks in a tongue edifies himself, but he who prophesies edifies the church. I wish you all spoke with tongues, but even more that you prophesied; for he who prophesies is greater than he who speaks with tongues, unless indeed he interprets, that the church may receive edification" (verses 2-5).

Someone who speaks in tongues speaks to God, while someone who prophesies speaks to others.

Verses 2-5 contrast prophecy and tongues, explaining that prophecy is more beneficial in public meetings than tongues, unless there is an interpretation for the latter. Someone who speaks in tongues speaks to God, while someone who prophesies speaks to others. Speaking in tongues benefits the speaker only, while prophecy benefits the entire congregation. Thus, in a group setting, prophecy is more valuable than tongues alone. If speaking in tongues is accompanied by interpretation, however, then it has the same value as prophecy.

"But now, brethren, if I come to you speaking with tongues, what shall I profit you unless I speak to you either by revelation, by knowledge, by prophesying, or by teaching? Even things without life, whether flute or harp, when they make a sound, unless they make a distinction in the sounds, how will it be known what is piped or played? For if the trumpet makes an uncertain sound, who will prepare himself for battle? So likewise you, unless you utter by the tongue words easy to understand, how will it be known what is spoken? For you will be speaking into the air. There are, it may be, so many kinds of languages in the world, and none of them is without significance. Therefore, if I do not know the meaning of the language, I shall be a foreigner to him who speaks, and he who speaks will be a foreigner to me" (verses 6-11).

These verses provide examples of the superiority of an understandable message. A flutist and a harpist must play distinct notes to create a song, and a military trumpeter or bugler must play distinct notes when issuing commands for battle. Likewise, when someone speaks to the church, he must use understandable speech to communicate, or else he is like a foreigner.

This discussion holds true both for the supernatural gift of prophecy and for prophecy in the general sense of all anointed speaking, including preaching. Verse 6 uses four words to describe an utterance in a known tongue. They are not necessarily mutually exclusive, but together they cover all types of spiritual speech in the church, whether revealed directly from God ("revelation") or acquired through the study of God's Word ("knowledge").

"Even so you, since you are zealous for spiritual gifts, let it be for the edification of the church that you seek to excel" (verse 12).

This sentence enunciates the principle of seeking the greatest good for the church. If we truly want to be spiritual, we should think about the needs of others. We should excel in ministry to the body.

Clearly this passage does not describe someone receiving the Holy Spirit or praying individually. It relates to group worship. Apparently, the Corinthian believers were so zealous for spiritual gifts that when they came together speaking in tongues dominated their corporate worship. They had plenty of other opportunities to speak in tongues for personal edification, however. They needed to use their valuable meeting time for something that would edify the body.

"Therefore let him who speaks in a tongue pray that he may interpret. For if I pray in a tongue, my spirit prays, but my understanding is unfruitful" (verses 13-14).

These verses provide the practical application

regarding tongues in a church service: If God moves on an individual to speak to the group in tongues, then he should pray for God to give him the interpretation. In this way he will be able to bless everyone rather than merely himself.

CONCLUSIONS REGARDING THE VOCAL GIFTS IN PUBLIC WORSHIP (I CORINTHIANS 14:15-25)

"What is the result then? I will pray with the spirit, and I will also pray with the understanding. I will sing with the spirit, and I will also sing with the understanding" (verse 15).

Here is the conclusion for the personal use of tongues: It is valuable to pray and sing in tongues, and it is valuable to pray and sing in one's own language. Both are important; neither should be disparaged or slighted. The implication is that each have their proper time and place.

"Otherwise, if you bless with the spirit, how will he who occupies the place of the uninformed say 'Amen' at your giving of thanks, since he does not understand what you say? For you indeed give thanks well, but the other is not edified. I thank my God I speak with tongues more than you all; yet in the church I would rather speak five words with my understanding, that I may teach others also, than ten

thousand words in a tongue" (verses 16-19).

These verses further elaborate on the distinction between the public and private uses of tongues, reiterating the thought of verses 1-14. If someone is called upon to pray a representative prayer, it is better to pray in the common language so that all can give informed assent to the prayer offered on their behalf (verses 16-17). Tongues is very valuable for personal devotion; indeed Paul would not let anyone outdo him in that regard (verse 18). Yet "in the church"—in meetings of believers—a few understandable words are more valuable than many unknown words (verse 19).

> *Tongues is very valuable*
> *for personal devotion.*

Verses 15-16 and verses 18-19 are parallel. Verse 15 and verse 18 both proclaim the value of tongues in private devotion. On the other hand, verse 16 and verse 19 illustrate the superiority of understandable speech in public worship activities.

"Brethren, do not be children in understanding; however, in malice be babes, but in understanding be mature" (verse 20).

Anyone who does not grasp these principles is spiritually immature. We should be childlike with regard to evil—such as hatred, ill will, and revenge—but in spiritual understanding we must be mature. (See Romans 16:19.)

"In the law it is written: 'With men of other tongues and other lips I will speak to this people; and yet, for all that, they will not hear Me,' says the Lord. Therefore tongues are for a sign, not to those who believe but to unbelievers; but prophesying is not for unbelievers but for those who believe" (verses 21-22).

To explain further the purpose of tongues, verse 21 quotes from Isaiah 28:11-12, and verse 22 reveals that this Old Testament passage is a type or a prophetic preview of speaking in tongues in the New Testament church. Specifically, a public utterance in tongues is a sign to unbelievers, whether unsaved people or Christians who have questions, discouragement, or doubt. Whereas they might easily discount or ignore a message in their own language, the miraculous utterance confronts them with the supernatural. They must decide: Is this message a fake, or is it a miracle from God? If the latter, what does God want me to do? The utterance in tongues arrests the attention of the unbeliever so that he will more seriously consider the interpretation that is to follow.

A college student majoring in finance visited our church in Austin on several occasions. He met a certified public accountant in our church and developed great respect for both his professionalism and his spirituality. One Sunday the accountant gave a public message in tongues, which was interpreted. Although the student had been somewhat skeptical, this miracle persuaded him that speaking in tongues was real. It was a convincing sign to an unbeliever.

Prophecy primarily benefits believers.

Prophecy, on the other hand, primarily benefits believers—those who are saved or who at least acknowledge the supernatural. They do not need tongues to convince them to believe the miraculous and to listen to God's message, although public tongues can still be an encouragement and confirmation to them.

"Therefore if the whole church comes together in one place, and all speak with tongues, and there come in those who are uninformed or unbelievers, will they not say that you are out of your mind? But if all prophesy, and an unbeliever or an uninformed person comes in, he is convinced by all, he is judged by all. And thus the secrets of his heart are revealed; and so, falling down on his face, he will worship God and report that God is truly among you" (verses 23-25).

Verses 23-25 make the direct application to public services—when "the whole church comes together in one place." Tongues without interpretation do not benefit the unbeliever or untaught person who attends. If everyone speaks in personal, devotional tongues throughout a public service, the unbeliever who is present does not learn anything but thinks everyone is crazy. But preaching, testimony, or the gift of prophecy in the known language will convict the unbeliever, reveal the secrets of his heart, and lead him to repentance and worship. Here we see the importance of using spiritual gifts to bless others and specifically to reach the lost.

At first glance verses 23-25 may appear to contradict verse 22, but they do not. Verse 22 speaks of the sign value of a public utterance in tongues that is followed by an interpretation. The utterance in tongues gets the unbeliever's attention, transforming him into a believer in the move of God. Then the interpretation instructs him. In this sense the interpretation is equivalent to prophecy. Both are beneficial for people who come to church as unbelievers but who open their hearts and minds in faith due to the manifestation of the Spirit.

Verses 23-25 contrast private, devotional tongues with prophecy, showing that the former are not profitable when they dominate a public service but the latter is. Verse 22 explains the valid purpose of tongues—functioning as a sign to unbelievers—when used properly in a service, while verse 23 explains the detriment of tongues—confusing unbelievers—when not used properly.

GUIDELINES FOR ORDER IN PUBLIC WORSHIP (I CORINTHIANS 14:26-40)

"How is it then, brethren? Whenever you come together, each of you has a psalm, has a teaching, has

a tongue, has a revelation, has an interpretation. Let all things be done for edification" (verse 26).

A typical New Testament church service may include worship songs, teachings, tongues, revelations (prophetic utterances), and interpretations. Those who minimize or oppose tongues today ignore this pattern for a service. Their worship services never contain some of these elements, so clearly their understanding and experience are faulty. This verse argues in favor of the gifts of the Spirit in public worship as long as they are exercised for the right purpose: edification (building up) of the body.

"If anyone speaks in a tongue, let there be two or at the most three, each in turn, and let one interpret. But if there is no interpreter, let him keep silent in church, and let him speak to himself and to God. Let two or three prophets speak, and let the others judge. But if anything is revealed to another who sits by, let the first keep silent. For you can all prophesy one by one, that all may learn and all may be encouraged" (verses 27-31).

Here we find practical guidelines for church meetings to ensure that the vocal spiritual gifts are exercised for the edification of the entire audience:

1. *In one meeting, allow two, or at most three, public utterances in tongues* (addressing the entire audience) (verse 27). While speaking in tongues is a notable sign to the unbeliever, three such utterances are

adequate to demonstrate God's miraculous power and to establish the sign. Further utterances add little of value and could become a distraction.

2. *After a public utterance in tongues, wait for an interpretation* (verse 27). Otherwise, the tongue does not benefit the audience.

3. *If no interpretation is forthcoming, the speaker should be quiet* (verse 28). He should not continue to address the audience in tongues, for he is not benefiting them, but he can continue to pray quietly in tongues for his own benefit.

4. *In one meeting, allow two, or at most three, public prophecies* (supernatural utterances in the known tongue to the entire audience) (verse 29). This amount is sufficient to communicate God's message for the occasion.

While God is infallible, no human being is.

5. *The listeners should evaluate all prophetic utterances* (verse 30). While God is infallible, no human being is. Therefore, any utterance from a human could be wholly or partially erroneous. As we discussed in chapter 13, each listener has the responsibility to discern whether a prophecy is from God and, if so, how it applies to his life. In this context, to judge does not mean to find fault, condemn, or object publicly. It simply means to evaluate the validity and relevance of the message.

If speaker and listener are both filled with and motivated by the Holy Spirit, the Spirit within the listener will bear witness that he has indeed heard a message from the Lord. If there is no such witness, the listener should consider whether he has been sensitive to the Spirit and whether he has felt what the rest of the church has felt. The following scriptural statements, although in somewhat different contexts, illustrate the principle that a mature believer should be able to discern the work of the Spirit: "The Spirit Himself bears witness with our spirit" (Romans 8:16). "Now we have received, not the spirit of the world, but the Spirit who is from God, that we might know the things that have been freely given to us by God. . . . But he who is spiritual judges all things" (I Corinthians 2:12, 15). "He who has an ear, let him hear what the Spirit says to the churches" (Revelation 2:7).

As we discussed in chapter 3, the authoritative standard by which we judge all things, including prophecies, is the Bible. Spiritual discernment is somewhat subjective, but the written Word is objective. If an utterance contradicts the Bible, we must always follow the latter.

6. *If there is more than one prophecy, the speakers should take turns* (verses 30-31). They should not vie for attention, nor should two people prophesy at once. After one person has prophesied and it is evident that a second person also has a prophecy, the first person should stop and let the other person continue. The body is blessed most when everyone has an opportunity both to speak and to listen. By hearing a variety of people prophesy, all can learn and be encouraged. Everyone can

potentially exercise this gift as God enables.

Of course, from the previous guidelines we learn that not everyone will be able to speak in one service. Over a period of time, however, everyone should have an opportunity to participate in some way in the life of the church by sharing a testimony, devotional thought, meaningful passage of Scripture, or special prophecy.

When verse 27 says, "Let one interpret," it simply means, "Let someone interpret." There is no requirement that if one person speaks in tongues a different person must interpret, for verse 13 instructs the speaker to "pray that he may interpret." Nor does verse 27 mean that only one person may interpret multiple utterances in tongues. An interpretation serves the same function as a prophecy; just as several people may prophesy, so several may speak in tongues and several may interpret.

"And the spirits of the prophets are subject to the prophets. For God is not the author of confusion but of peace, as in all the churches of the saints" (verses 32-33).

The gift is subject to proper use or misuse, and it is our responsibility to use it properly.

Verse 32 affirms that we can abide by the foregoing rules, and verse 33 explains why these rules are necessary. As we discussed in chapter 4, when God gives us a gift, He does not eliminate our human will or override our freedom of choice. The gift is subject to proper use or misuse, and it is our responsibility to use it properly. If someone prays fervently until he speaks in tongues, God will not stop that utterance just because the circumstances are not appropriate. The speaker must regulate it according to the principles of God's Word. When he does so, he does not quench the Spirit, but he makes proper use of the gift and the choice God has given him.

Let us suppose God gives someone a prophetic message. The individual still must decide if the message is exclusively for his benefit, for another individual, or for the whole church. He must also decide when is the appropriate time to give it. Even when he correctly discerns God's purpose and timing, he must cooperate with the spiritual leadership of the church so as not to cause disruption or confusion.

In every church, God is more interested in peace, unity, cooperation, and mutual submission than in the exact timing and delivery of a certain prophecy. God can accomplish the purpose of a prophecy in many ways and times and through various people, but He never approves of disorder, contention, or rebellion. Thus the speaker of a prophecy can and must learn to control his own spirit so that he speaks in the manner and time that will edify the body.

"Let your women keep silent in the churches, for they are not permitted to speak; but they are to be submissive, as the law also says. And if they want to

learn something, let them ask their own husbands at home; for it is shameful for women to speak in church" (verses 34-35).

Verses 34-35 deal with another problem that was causing confusion in the meetings of the Corinthian saints. No only did the indiscriminate, unregulated speaking of tongues cause disruption, but so did the disorderly questions of some women in the church.

We can only guess at the exact nature of the problem, but apparently some Corinthian women were interrupting services by calling out questions. In those days, women usually did not receive a formal education as men did. In public meetings, men had the right to question a speaker publicly, but women did not. It could be that Christian women in Corinth were reveling in their new freedom in Christ to such an extent that they violated this social custom by questioning the preacher during his message when they did not understand something he said. Or it could be that in church meetings the men sat in one area and the women in another, just as in Orthodox Jewish synagogues today, and the women would call out to their husbands when they had questions.

In any case, the solution to the problem was for women to keep quiet in church and ask their questions of their husbands at home. By disrupting the service, they were bringing shame to themselves and dishonoring the leadership of their husbands.

Some people interpret the admonition for women to keep silent as an absolute prohibition, forbidding women to preach or prophesy, but both the immediate context and the whole of Scripture dispel this notion. In the context, women's keeping silent in church is coupled with asking questions of their husbands at home, showing that the prohibition relates to being noisy in church by not depending on their husbands to answer their questions.

I Corinthians 11:5 explains that women cannot pray or prophesy with their heads uncovered. The corollary is that if they have the covering of long hair (I Corinthians 11:15), thereby acknowledging the leadership of their husbands, then they can pray and prophesy in public worship. Indeed I Corinthians 14:31 says, "For you can all prophesy one by one," making no distinction between male and female in this regard. Moreover, the Book of Acts specifically states that, in accordance with God's plan for the latter days, women did prophesy in the early church (Acts 2:17; 21:9).

I Timothy 2:11-12 also teaches that a woman should be silent in church. Again, this statement is not an absolute prohibition, but in the context it forbids women from taking the leadership role away from men and becoming authoritative teachers over them. Both testaments show that, under the overall direction of men, women can fulfill many leadership roles in God's kingdom. Deborah was a judge of Israel, and she, as well as Huldah and Isaiah's wife, was also a prophetess (Judges 4:4; II Chronicles 34:22; Isaiah 8:3). Phoebe was a "servant" (Greek, *diakonos*, perhaps in the technical sense of "deaconess") of the church in Cenchrea. Priscilla, along with her husband, Aquila, was one of Paul's coworkers and taught a Bible study to the "Baptist" preacher Apollos (Acts 18:26; Romans 16:3). Other female gospel workers were Persis, Tryphena, and Tryphosa (Romans 16:12), and Junia was even considered an apostle along with Andronicus, probably her husband (Romans 16:7).

"Or did the word of God come originally from you? Or was it you only that it reached? If anyone thinks himself to be a prophet or spiritual, let him acknowledge that the things which I write to you are the commandments of the Lord. But if anyone is ignorant, let him be ignorant" (verses 36-38).

Here, the inspired apostle anticipated the probable response of some immature Christians to the instructions of this chapter: "But I am spiritual, and I can't quench the Spirit. I am a prophet, and God gave me a message to deliver regardless of your rules. God spoke to me before He spoke to you. In fact, He spoke to me instead of you!" Paul issued an apostolic rebuke to those who think this way. Truly spiritual people will recognize the need for order in the church, for submission to leadership, and for careful exercise of gifts to ensure benefit to the whole body. They will recognize that these commandments have come from God Himself. Anyone who rejects these guidelines will remain spiritually immature and ignorant.

"Therefore, brethren, desire earnestly to prophesy, and do not forbid to speak with tongues. Let all

things be done decently and in order" (verses 39-40).

Verses 39-40 summarize the teaching of the chapter, providing in a nutshell the solution to the problem of disruption in the Corinthian church. The Corinthians were not lacking in spiritual gifts and manifestations, but as we see throughout the epistle they were lacking in maturity and unity. (See, for example, I Corinthians 1:10-13; 3:1-4.) The most important spiritual manifestations they needed were prophecies—understandable messages to the whole church that would strengthen the body. Instead of additional individual manifestations, they needed gifts that would enhance unity and lead to a maturity characterized by concern and consideration for one another.

In corporate meetings,
our primary goals must be
to worship God, to hear from God,
and to minister to one another.

Here we find an important principle of general application: In corporate meetings, in addition to worshiping God our primary goals must be to hear from God and to minister to one another. We need to pray for God to speak to us collectively through prophecy in every sense of the word—anointed preaching, teaching, and testimony as well as supernatural utterances directly from God in the local language. We also need tongues with interpretation, which together provide the same benefit as prophecy.

While emphasizing the most needed gifts in public worship, Paul, unlike many commentators today, did not disparage or discourage any spiritual gift. In trying to bring order to chaotic services, he did not want anyone to conclude that he opposed gifts such as tongues. He did not want anyone to misconstrue or misapply his instructions so as to forbid public utterances in tongues, whether in theory or in practice. He simply wanted to make sure that all public utterances were for the benefit of everybody.

Finally, whatever we do in public worship, it should be decent and orderly. The Greek word translated "decently" is *euschemonos*, which comes from *euschemon*, meaning "decorous, proper, noble, honorable." The adjective appears in I Corinthians 7:35 and 12:24, where the NKJV translates it respectively as "proper" and "presentable." We should not allow confusion, chaos, rebellion, or selfishness, but everything we do should be for the good of the body.

Each of us has a responsibility to fulfill this admonition in our local church. The pastor is ultimately responsible to guide the church correctly. The leader of the service is responsible to follow the leading of the Spirit, not quenching the Spirit but also not allowing violations of the scriptural guidelines we have discussed. Typically, disorderly situations can be handled tactfully by promoting group worship, by changing the order of the service, or, if need be, by speaking a few words of public or private instruction. On rare occasions, a public pastoral rebuke is necessary to counteract a demonic or carnal influence that seeks to dominate the service.

The responsibility of each member is to follow the guidelines that have been given, to be sensitive to the Spirit, and to follow the direction of the pastor and service leader. A mature congregation can overcome any negative spiritual influences and unite together to achieve spiritual victory in a church.

We can summarize the entire teaching on spiritual gifts in I Corinthians 12-14 by the principles we find in the last two verses. *First*, we should earnestly desire all the gifts of the Spirit, particularly those that will benefit the whole church under the particular circumstances. *Second*, we should not forbid or discourage any spiritual gift, as long as it is used to bless everyone. *Finally*, we should conduct all spiritual activities in a decent and orderly manner so as to fulfill the supreme objectives of glorifying Jesus Christ and edifying His body.

CONCLUSION

God "is able to do exceedingly abundantly above all that we ask or think, according to the power that works in us" (Ephesians 3:20). May we who are filled with the Holy Spirit recognize the supernatural potential that rests in us and allow God's Spirit to flow through us. Our God is not distant; He is present in our lives with miraculous power. When we have the Holy Spirit, we have the author of all nine spiritual gifts resident within us, and He can activate any that we need.

Let us exercise simple faith to receive God's miraculous gifts, and let us stir up the gifts He has already placed in our midst. Whenever needs arise, we should believe His Word and believe that He can work through us. His power is at work "in us"; we must let it flow through us to meet the needs. In this way the gifts of the Spirit will become vital tools for strengthening the saints and reaching the lost with the gospel of Jesus Christ.

About the Author

DAVID K. BERNARD is the founder and pastor of New Life United Pentecostal Church of Austin, Texas, the associate editor in the Editorial Division of the United Pentecostal Church International, and a member of the Texas District Board. A former college professor and a member of the State Bar of Texas, he holds a doctorate of jurisprudence with honors from the University of Texas and a bachelor's degree *magna cum laude* in mathematical sciences and managerial studies from Rice University. He also studied Greek at Wesley Biblical Seminary. His books have been published in twenty languages, and he has ministered in many countries on five continents. He is listed in *Who's Who in Religion* and *Who's Who in U.S. Writers, Editors and Poets*. He and his wife, Connie, have three children: Jonathan, Daniel, and Lindsey.

Other Books by DAVID K. BERNARD

Order from:
Pentecostal Publishing House
8855 Dunn Road
Hazelwood, MO 63042-2299